Praise for *Still Growing*

Kirk Cameron is a fresh and honest voice in today's Christian culture. *Still Growing* is a surefire hit!

Karen Kingsbury
New York Times bestselling author, *Between Sundays* and *Ever After*

It's amazing how our beliefs lead us! Kirk takes us on a whirlwind tour of the amazing peaks and the despairing valleys of his life with sincerity, vulnerability and passion. His choice to choose faith at the height of his career is a model for every person! I heartily recommend *Still Growing*.

Gary Smalley
Bestselling author, *Change Your Heart, Change Your Life*

STILL GROWING

STILL GROWING

An Autobiography

kirk
cameron

with Lissa Halls Johnson

Regal

From Gospel Light
Ventura, California, U.S.A.

Published by Regal

From Gospel Light

Ventura, California, U.S.A.

www.regalbooks.com

Printed in the U.S.A.

All Scripture quotations, unless otherwise indicated, are taken from the *New American Standard Bible,* © 1960, 1962, 1963, 1968, 1971, 1972, 1973, 1975, 1977 by The Lockman Foundation. Used by permission. All others are the author's paraphrase.

Library of Congress Cataloging-in-Publication Data

Cameron, Kirk, 1970-

Still growing / Kirk Cameron.

p. cm.

ISBN 978-0-8307-4451-0 (hard cover)

1. Cameron, Kirk, 1970- 2. Evangelists—United States—Biography.

3. Actors—United States--Biography. I. Title.

BV3785.C25A3 2008

269'.2092—dc22

[B]

2008000600

1 2 3 4 5 6 7 8 9 10 / 15 14 13 12 11 10 09 08

Rights for publishing this book outside the U.S.A. or in non-English languages are administered by Gospel Light Worldwide, an international not-for-profit ministry. For additional information, please visit www.glww.org, email info@glww.org, or write to Gospel Light Worldwide, 1957 Eastman Avenue, Ventura, CA 93003, U.S.A.

Contents

Acknowledgments

It would be impossible to write a book like this—with honesty and multiple perspectives—without the help of family and friends who saw the events from their own vantage points and workmates who knew the inside scoop better than I, many of whom were willing to be interviewed, poked and prodded to recollect what it was *really* like back in the day. Thanks to my dad and mom, sisters, grandparents, aunts, uncles, friends and co-workers who were willing to open their memory banks and share what's there—all for a good read.

My sincere thanks to my friend Lissa Halls Johnson for her invaluable work co-writing this book. Without her many hours of questioning, researching, brainstorming and creative writing, it wouldn't have gotten done. Her talent and hard work is what brought my story to life.

Thanks to my amazing and wonderful wife, who is endlessly patient with me, and whose support, encouragement and discernment made this project not only possible, but fun to work on.

I'm beyond grateful for my children, whose real lives have given me lots of fun stories to tell. They make me want to be a better father and husband.

I'm continually grateful to Mark Craig, my manager, for his genuine friendship and tremendous support of my family, career and ministry.

My gratitude to Ray Comfort for his partnership in the gospel and encouragement to "do it now!"

To Dan Ewald, my talented friend who saved the day and helped me find the "funny" in my life—thank you.

And to my Lord and Savior Jesus Christ—You are the pearl of great price.

I am indebted to you all.

Kirk

Chapter 1

On Top of the World

1987

I reached for the rubber knob on my cassette player and cranked Prince to the max. He was singing about purple rain, but the L.A. skies were a clear blue that sunny day. I was flyin' down the freeway in my new Honda 2.0 SI Prelude, the wind giving even more bounce to my already afro'd mullet.

I grinned, remembering the cruel pleasure of deceiving Tracey Gold yet again. Not that it was hard to do—Tracey was the most gullible person in the world. Just last week while carpooling to the studio I had started in on her.

"This car's got the sweetest technology, Trace," I bragged. "It's so smart, all you have to do is set it on automatic pilot and it drives itself."

"Shut up. Does not," she furrowed her brow.

"Does so. This car has special radars. It can read the lanes and stay within the lines. It also slows down when it senses a car ahead."

Tracey's eyes widened and her mouth gaped. *"Really?"*

I flipped a non-existent switch on the far side of the steering column just out of sight, put my hands behind my head and guided the wheel with my left knee. "See?"

She bought it. "Wow. That's amazing!"

It was classic Carol and Mike Seaver. If I had told that story to the writers, they probably would have written it into the show.

But enough reminiscing. Prince was singing and it seemed disrespectful not to focus on every last word. He was, hands down, my favorite rock star. My dressing room sported purple light bulbs alternating with the standard marquee bulbs around the mirror. Posters were tacked to violet-painted walls of Prince straddling his 'cycle, a curvy Latina babe perched behind him, his cape billowing in the breeze.

The tape ran out and I fumbled around the cassette rack for my Boy George tape. I enjoyed crooning along with "I'll Tumble for Ya," even though Boy was a he-she who wore pastel eye shadow. Maybe it didn't seem strange to me because my day job also required wearing pancake make-up—or *man-cake*, as I preferred to call it.

It was the '80s, and it was the best time to be a kid: mastering the Rubik's Cube in speed contests, getting joystick-cramp in that spot between your thumb and index finger from hours of playing Donkey Kong and Berzerk, growing a Chia Pet (which kind of resembled my own hair) . . . I could go on.

Everything was big. Big colors, big belts, big glasses, big boom boxes.

Without realizing it, I was setting trends (well, my *stylists* were setting trends). I didn't know the first thing about fashion. If someone had given me a tank top with shoulder pads, I probably would have put it on. I couldn't possibly have understood the influence I had—or, to be honest, the influence my character, Mike Seaver, had. When I spun around sporting sunglasses and a brown leather coat during the *Growing Pains* theme, millions of teens were doing the same thing in front of their bathroom mirrors. I had no idea.

Boy George started a new tune as I exited the Pass Avenue ramp off the 101 and headed towards the Warner Bros. Ranch. This part of the drive was often the most entertaining. I took great pleasure in leaving my window down and maneuvering up to a red light next to a car filled with girls. I'd glance over, flashing my famously crooked smile.

"Morning, ladies."

I loved the double takes, the ear-piercing screams. Without fail, their spastic hands fluttered while their lips mouthed my name. The best part was taking off while the shock kept them stuck in the intersection.

The previous night during taping, I found another way to stroke my ego. A girl had won a chance to play a bit part on the show, though she had been told I wouldn't be around for the scene. An older man playing her father said his lines and all went normally. But when the second take rolled around, I snuck in and said the father's lines. The girl grabbed her stomach, shaking all over. She stared, incredulous, while I soaked up every moment of her ecstatic squeals. When I hugged her, I thought she'd pass out in my arms.

With a wave to the security guard, I pulled my car into the parking space marked "For Kirk Cameron Only" next to Stage 30. I jumped out and headed to my 30-foot motor home. Another day, another 10 grand.

It cracked me up: *me*, a celebrity? I was told I was a "heartthrob," which sounded like a condition a person should have checked by a medical professional. Teen mags plastered my mug on their covers, with modest centerfold pictures inside. Q&As covered my fave color (purple), my fave shows (*Family Ties* and *Cosby*), my height (5' 7"), weight (130 pounds) and eye color (hazel). They also printed false information. One said my parents were a psychologist and a newspaper reporter. Sure, my *television* parents held those careers—my *real* parents were a math/P.E. teacher and a housewife/manager (of me).

I was supposed to be the coolest kid on the planet, but no one knew what a dork I was.

I received 10,000 letters per week, mostly from girls who wanted to meet me, touch me, marry me. I had a fan club that sent out a variety of keepsakes—photos, T-shirts, buttons, even a pillowcase with my picture just the right size for girls to kiss my fabric-y likeness as they drifted off to sleep. *Weird.*

Wherever I went people catered to me. Limousines carted me off to the next gig. Waiters comped my meals. Flight attendants whispered, "Mr. Cameron, why don't you come with me?" and escorted me to first class. Once off the plane, people laid down a red carpet and greeted me on the tarmac with military-like fanfare.

When I arrived at a party, everyone sat up and took notice. The room buzzed with not-so-quiet whispers: "Isn't that Kirk Cameron?" The adoration was obvious in the body language, facial expressions and eagerness of those around me. All of it baffled me beyond belief. I was in the midst of a phenomenon I felt I had no hand in creating.

I had everything the rest of the world craved—money, fame, fortune, any girl I wanted. I admit, I liked that part. What 16-year-old guy didn't want girls to melt when he walked in the room? And I certainly wasn't complaining when Domino's Pizza offered me a million bucks to be their ad boy.

If I didn't have something, it was only because I didn't want it. I was a devout atheist, livin' large, hanging out with the beautiful people.

Years later when people asked about that time in my life, I defined it like this: Imagine a world where whatever you want is given to you as quickly as possible. When you walk into a room, all the adults smile at you, talk nicely and say, "What do you want? Okay, I'll give that to you."

Everything in your life is carefully placed with the intent to make you happy. If you aren't happy, no expense is too great in order to fix the situation. As far as you can tell, you are the center of the universe. Everything revolves around you, your schedule, your dreams and wishes. You are more important to adults than other kids are. "Why is that?" your little mind asks. And the only answer you can come up with is that you are *very, very* unique.

That was my childhood, my adolescence, my reality.

The smug 16-year-old climbing out of his white Honda Prelude had no time to muse about what was wrong with that picture. I was Kirk Cameron, and I was on top of the world.

Chapter 2

Fear and Loathing

1988

I paced the floor of my dressing room, palms pressed hard against my temples. I was trying to escape the noise inside my head. My stomach churned as if I'd downed some bad orange juice.

Please don't make me do this.

I pressed my hands tighter, trying to squeeze out the angst and frustration.

If only . . .

To the outside, it would have seemed ironic that a television star envied by millions could be here pacing, distraught and alone in his dressing room.

Confrontation had never been my thing. That's why I had agents—slick suits who enjoyed negotiating a higher salary, bigger perks, more respect. But this wasn't something they would do for me. They wouldn't understand. They *couldn't* understand. If I had tried to tell them what I was about to do they would have said that I was over-reacting and was going to ruin my career.

"Let it go, Kirk," they would have insisted. "Do your job. Give 'em that million-dollar smile and don't blow it. Get to syndication and we'll *all* be multi-millionaires."

I was a peace-loving guy by nature. I prided myself on being a devilish clown, laughing his way through life and using that optimistic outlook to lighten the burdens of others. But I couldn't chuckle my way through this one.

I had to figure out a way to get my point across without offending the producers. I needed to be a man, even though I wasn't quite one—

at least not legally. I was just a 17-year-old kid who wanted to do the right thing. And I knew that no matter how I tried to camouflage, soften or sweet-talk it, someone would be unhappy, maybe even furious, by what I had to say. I hated the lose-lose place I found myself in. I *hated* it.

I opened my eyes and saw the glow of my over-priced Swatch. (Again, the '80s.) I didn't have much time left. I needed to do this or let it go.

I took a deep breath and got a drink of water to strengthen myself for what was ahead. I didn't want my voice to do that Mike Seaver puberty-crack or my bosses would have a difficult time taking my concerns seriously.

I stood in front of the mirror to practice my speech. No one was here to tell me how to say my lines as my mom did when I was younger. I didn't have a writer handing me lines to make me witty and resolve everything at the end of 23.5 minutes. I didn't have a director to tell me the right way to look, the right emotion to portray or the right inflection to get the desired response from my audience.

I ran my fingers through my curly mullet, trying to mess it up so I didn't look too Hollywood-slick. I gripped the sides of the sink and took a deep breath. *I am an actor. I can do this,* I told myself, loosening my neck by performing a few head rolls. *Kirk, you've gotta make a choice. Are you going to do what you think is right or are you gonna compromise?*

"I want to do the right thing," I answered aloud, like an overly earnest character in an after-school special.

But what was the right thing? Letting the show go on, as written? Or stepping in, hoping that I could—in a respectful way—point out how things could be different? It would be a mistake to remind producers what they already knew—that a TV series has an unspoken agreement with its audience to be what it has been from the beginning. A sitcom shouldn't become a drama. Nobody wants to see a homicide investigation on *Mr. Belvedere.* (On *Murphy Brown,* maybe.) A show about a middle-class suburban family shouldn't suddenly focus on illegal immigrants and their struggle to cross the border.

My inner voice kept reminding me that I was just a kid, while the producers were authority figures—albeit odd authority figures. As a child actor, I had learned early that I wielded more power than most adults, yet my parents instilled within me a respect and a desire to submit to authority. My parents never put up with the typical child-star behavior. At the same time, I was taught to speak firmly, as an adult, to these powerful figures who had the ability to turn my life into a Hollywood game. I needed to walk the fine line of standing up for my convictions and respecting authority.

Pacing, I tried to find words to express how I felt about the new direction of *Growing Pains*. It felt as though we were straying from what made our show successful: the fact it was a wholesome family show.

I cleared my throat and tried again. "Hey, guys," I said to the make-up mirror, trying to muster my most sincere smile. "How ya doin'? How was your weekend?"

The hardest part would be to explain my motives. I knew how others would see it. I knew the quiet uproar it would cause. Tension on the set would thicken. The producers and writers would be irritated. The cast and crew would roll their eyes or glare at me over the stupidity of what I was asking. Maybe some would try to understand, but most wouldn't.

Most would think I was flaunting my celebrity.

No matter what I said or did, that would be the fallout. No matter how I tried to share my true heart, the assumption in "the business" would be that I was messing with the status quo as a power play.

Power-tripping had never been me. Fame and celebrity didn't come naturally. I really didn't like star-struck fans following me with their mouths agape, watching everything I did as if I were a freak. I wanted to be a normal teenage kid with an unusual job. I wanted to be seen for *me*, not given higher status as a human being just because I'd landed a part on a hit show.

I leaned my forehead against the door, wishing I could just let it go so that we could be the happy cast and crew we'd always been. But something had happened to me and I no longer saw life the same way.

In the early years of the show, I had earned a reputation as the prankster who planted stink bombs under the audience seats, greased doorknobs and hid crew members' cars in bushes. I initiated practical jokes, laughter, ribbing and the sarcastic comments that flew around stage like the evil monkeys on *The Wizard of Oz*. My fellow cast members affectionately named me "Devil Boy."

But I had recently become a new man. I had stepped from the house that had fallen from the twister and it had changed my entire world from black-and-white to Technicolor. Once there, no matter what Dorothy or the Wizard said, I realized I couldn't go back.

"Is it wrong to bring my new convictions to the set?" I asked myself. "Should I keep them wrapped up inside, letting business be business? After all, TV isn't real. A sitcom is just a *story*. And the stories aren't real. The characters aren't real, either."

Now I sounded like a crazy person, talking to myself in my dressing room.

I knew Mike Seaver wasn't me and I wasn't him, but viewers didn't seem to know the difference. To them, the Seavers existed. If Mike took drugs, kids would assume it was okay to take drugs—all because Mike was cool and someone to follow.

I didn't want to blow it. That would be my nightmare. I desperately wanted to do the right thing in a no-win situation. I knew people would be unhappy with me. But it was something I had to do . . . and the time was now.

Chapter 3

The Making of Kirk Cameron

I am so much like my mom. In her book, *A Full House of Growing Pains*, she says, "I was raised to be a good girl. And I *was* a good girl. Unlike some kids, I really *wanted* to be good . . . Like many kids who want to be good, I was influenced in part by my desire-to-please personality, in part by my strict parental upbringing."[1]

That was me from the earliest I can remember. I wanted to please people and make them happy. If an adult had told me to jump off a cliff I would have replied, "Leading with my left foot or right?"

I formed my choices around what would please others around me. I wanted to be good—but more than that, I wanted to *do the right thing*. Whatever the cost to me or others, I wanted to do what was right. I hated letting people down, hated thinking I'd hurt someone. (Well, excluding my sisters. That was my job and I did it with zeal.)

An Idyllic Start

I wanted to be a fireman, astronaut or doctor when I grew up. Combining all three would have been ideal—a man equally equipped to control an engine fire in the shuttle and to provide medical services to life forms found on Mars, all at zero gravity. My face would be in the encyclopedia under the listing *Astrofirector*.

Sadly, my parents grounded my career aspirations by choosing to live on Earth, in the San Fernando Valley home they reside in to this day. Robert Cameron and Barbara Bausmith met on a Santa Monica beach one Sunday afternoon about a million years ago. Dad was trying to be cool, even though he had a huge safety pin holding up his orange swim trunks. Mom thought he was funny, playful and cute. That he was seven years older and a math teacher impressed her, though the safety pin wasn't doing him any favors. The moment she saw him jump into the driver's seat of a white Mustang convertible with a bunch of guys, she was smitten. It wasn't until their first date when he picked her up in a Volkswagen Beetle that she discovered he'd bribed his cousin to let him pretend the Mustang was his car. She went out with him anyway, and before the year was up she proposed to him. He accepted and they were off to an interesting start to a relationship that has never ceased to be anything but.

> I was raised to be a good girl. And I was a good girl. Unlike some kids, I really wanted to be good . . . Like many kids who want to be good, I was influenced in part by my desire-to-please personality, in part by my strict parental upbringing.
>
> Barbara Cameron, Kirk's mom

They didn't waste time having kids. I was born October 12, 1970, and was named for my dad's hero, Captain Kirk of the *Starship Enterprise*. Mom only agreed because Kirk meant "of the Church." She decided that was a pretty good legacy to put on a kid—even if she didn't go to church herself.

Bridgette followed less than a year later. They took a breather before Melissa arrived in 1974, and Candace came 18 months later in 1976.

I wasn't raised in a Christian home, but it was a moral home. My parents stood on old-fashioned family values, like the difference between right and wrong: You didn't lie, smoke, do drugs, drink alcohol or have sex outside of marriage.

As a little girl, Mom had a simple faith in God, which began in church and shaped many of her values and decisions. When she married Dad, she presumed they would go to church as a family—but Dad had other ideas. He didn't want his kids being corralled into any particular religion. He insisted his kids be able to make up their own minds when they were older, so he adamantly refused to let us attend even Sunday school. So Mom kept quiet and prayed in the simple way she knew how.

We were never allowed to play alone. We had to be in when the street lights went on. We could play with our cousins, aunts, uncles, grandparents and with the Rock family (no relation to the wrestler). The Rocks were our parents' best friends, and their two boys, Ryan and Andrew, pretty much rounded out our play circle. We had a blast—never a dull moment.

Dad refurbished old juke boxes, one a 1948 Rock-Ola bubbler with neon tubes running around the outside. He glued 45s back-to-back so they'd play only the best songs—never the dull flip sides. We cranked those puppies, singing and dancing to the music of the '50s, '60s and '70s. My sisters and I were probably the only kids who knew the lyrics to "Eight-Eyed Emily." The whole family joined in the dancing, though Mom preferred to sit and watch—she was our most enthusiastic audience.

My Aunt Joanne (Mom's sister) was married to David Cameron (Dad's brother). I loved going over to their house because they were less strict than my parents and had a yard designed for kids. They had built a winding cement sidewalk perfect for bikes, trikes and roller skates. They had a wading pool, a trampoline, a zip line and chickens. Who needed amusement parks?

Aunt Joanne and Uncle David were hippie-like. They kept a compost pile, which I thought was cool. They grew their own grapes that they crushed by stomping on them in five-gallon drums—tubes traversed from one drum to the other, and the sludge eventually became wine. (It's still gross to think about my Uncle David's feet on those grapes.) They ate really healthy stuff—we'd have sprout sandwiches, tahini on whole wheat bread with sprouts and avocado. I always liked it . . . but then again, I was a health-conscious weirdo.

I was also fascinated with the scientific world, so Aunt Joanne took me on hikes where we cast animal prints in plaster of Paris. We made tin foil toy boats using kebob skewers for masts and bubblegum to hold it all together. We played "how many kids can we pile on a tandem bike and still ride it?" in the cul-de-sac. Always creative, Aunt Joanne and Uncle David took us to a local park, strapped our skates on, pinned a bed-sheet corner to a knee of our Toughskin jeans while we held another corner. Off we'd fly as the wind blew us down the sidewalk.

Our families went camping in Yosemite together, where we floated down the river on inner tubes, laughing and teasing all the way down. I couldn't get enough of Aunt Joanne.

Beach Sundays

Beach Sundays were foundational to the history of the Cameron family. Nothing topped those days. We woke up jazzed, running around shouting, "We're going to the beach! We're going to the beach!" Dad had breakfast ready at 6:30.

Then he designated teams—me and Bridgette, Melissa and Candace, me and Candace, whatever. Team One was the prep team and had the job of making lunches (tuna sandwiches, Wheat Thins, apricots, Oreos, water) and packing the van. (Aunt Joanne's girls liked our food better because we "brought the good stuff.") The Igloo, folding chairs, umbrella, Frisbees, beach towels and boogie boards were carted to the Volkswagen van.

Team Two had the worst job. After a day at the beach, they—tired, sticky, with sand in every crevasse—had to empty the van and clean it. It took much longer to perform these dreaded tasks, the sun having sapped all our energy and motivation for living.

There were two ways to get to the beach: the canyon or the freeway. We hated the freeway because it seemed so much longer; we preferred driving through Malibu Canyon and Topanga Canyon. I don't know why—as anyone who has ever followed a Volkswagen van can attest, those engines have no power. We poked and sputtered along the steep, winding roads, willing the van to make it over the hill just one more time. It might have been faster to cut holes in the bottom for our legs, *Flintstones*-style.

Dad barely got the van stopped at Sorrento Beach when four tow-headed kids fell out all over each other, eager to get the day going. We waited impatiently for him to hand over the items for us to carry over the endless hot sand. (It was probably only a quarter-mile wide, but our legs were short and stubby.) We ran as fast as we could until it felt like our feet would blister, threw a towel on the sand and stood on it until our feet cooled, then picked up and took off until we hit water.

Aunt Joanne was there first, with a million towels to stake out our massive territory. There were always hugs and kisses all around, even if we'd just seen each other the day before.

I knew I was lucky to have both sets of grandparents there every week—Frank and Jeanne, and George and Helen. Grandma Helen wore pants, a shirt and long gloves that covered her hands and sat under an umbrella so she wouldn't get burned.

I don't remember Mom ever wearing a bathing suit, though she must have. She felt self-conscious, always thinking she was fat.

I had my own issues. I was self-conscious about taking my shirt off. I was born with my sternum concave in the middle of my chest. People would make fun of me: "What happened to you? You got a hole in your chest!" They nicknamed me "Indent." I wanted to hide this embarrassing deformity, so I chose to lie face down on the towel. (This would come up later when a magazine editor wanted this "teen hunk" to take a cheesy picture with an unzipped leather coat and no shirt underneath. So embarrassing.)

Dad was a really good body surfer, and so was his father. For years I watched them go way out into the water, then catch waves and ride them all the way in.

"Dad," I asked one day, "will you teach me to body surf?"

"You bet, Baby Buck. Come over here. This is what you do."

He showed me how to hold my head up, paste my arms against my sides and point my toes. He helped me figure out where on the crest of the wave I'd get the best ride. He took me out so deep, I had to tread water until the right one came.

"This one!" he'd shout. "Okay. Wait. Wait. *Go!*"

And off I shot toward the shore. I hated when I caught it wrong and the wave tumbled me over and over until I was so disoriented that I had no idea which way was up. Just as I thought my lungs would burst I'd pop out of the water, usually dumped on the sand by the retreating wave.

One summer, with Grandpa George's instruction, we decided to make our own skim boards. We beveled the bottoms and found a beach-y image to polyurethane on the top. We mixed a catalyst with a resin to cover the whole thing, making it really slick.

I took my 20-pound board and threw it on the sand just as a wave began to retreat, leaving a thin layer of water. As the board began to skim across the water, I jumped on and slid across the sand. If I dared to ride to the wave, it would toss me in the air like a rag doll. But if I did it just right, I could do flips and other tricks.

Uncle Frankie loved to create "professional" fights between me and Bridgette. He drew a little fighting ring in the sand while Bridgette did a little pre-fight dance in her corner and I did one in mine.

Frankie held Bridgette's hand high in the air and shouted in perfect announcer-voice, "In *this* corner we have Bridgette Cameron weighing in at 45 pounds. She's the leanest, meanest, scrappiest fighter you've ever seen!" Then he grabbed my wrist: "And in *this* corner we have Kirk Cameron, weighing in at 55 pounds . . . the heavyweight champion of the world!"

At *Ding! Ding!* we started wrestling. For me it was just goofy fun, but for Bridgette this was serious stuff—a chance to get back at me for all the pranks I pulled on her. Inevitably, someone would throw sand in somebody else's face, and Bridgette would get so mad that she abandoned the rules and started swingin'. The intense look on her face sapped my killer boxing skills as I buckled in laughter. I laughed so hard I couldn't defend myself. She knew the secret of my strength and used it to pummel the life out of me.

On exceptionally good Sundays, Dad stopped at Foster's Freeze on the way home. The best treat in the world was a soft-serve vanilla cone dipped in chocolate at the end of a perfect day at the beach.

Aunt Joanne

I really didn't like being the center of attention—strange for a kid who became the center of attention everywhere he went, eh? I often wanted to melt into the floor so people wouldn't see me.

One day I was at Aunt Joanne's. She had dyed a mop-head blue and parted it down the middle so it looked like a blue wig. She also had a pair of big goofy glasses.

"Hey, Kirk," she said as she got down on my level. "Want to do something fun?"

I looked at her, not wanting to commit just yet.

She brought the wig out from behind her back. "Why don't we put this mop and glasses on? I'd love to take your picture."

I shook my head, terrified someone would see me in that ridiculous get-up. I knew it would certainly bring unwanted attention.

> Five was a very interesting age for Kirk. He was very bright and would analyze situations before becoming involved. You could see in his eyes that he was trying to take it all in and make sense of it; if it was something he trusted or not. If he wasn't comfortable, he wouldn't get involved. . . . He didn't voice his opinion, you could just tell by how he hung back. . . . He didn't like putting himself out in front. It was almost like if somebody wanted to praise him, or dote on him, or say, "Come here, you're so cute," he wanted nothing to do with that. So he would just go into another room or go outside. He'd just disappear.
>
> Aunt Joanne Cameron

She kept talking: "Kirk, this is so funny, it's just you and me. No one else will ever see this picture."

I inwardly wanted to do it, but I didn't want anyone to point and say, "Look! How cute!" or whatever dumb things adults might say. And what if the kids laughed at me?

Aunt Joanne reassured me. "I don't want to embarrass you, Kirk. I only want to take this picture. It will be fun."

"Okay," I agreed, hesitantly.

Aunt Joanne put the glasses on my face combed down the blue bangs.

"Hurry," I pushed.

She backed up and readied the camera.

I stood there stiff, like a soldier. I thought, *Take the stinkin' picture so I can get out of this!*

Once the flash went off, I started pulling on the wig. "Okay. We've done it. I'm done." (About 12 years later I donned a friend's underwear on my head like a helmet—the leg holes for my eyes—and marched into a restaurant, where all eyes turned on me. Even at that age, I claimed to dislike undo attention unless it was on *my terms*. Unfortunately, celebrity brought attention on everyone else's terms—like the time a guy approached me at the urinal, mid-stream, and asked for my autograph.)

Grandparents

I only wanted affection on my terms as well, and my grandparents knew it. One day I was at Grandma Jeanne's house, tormenting my sisters. Three times the girls ran inside to tattle on me. Grandma called me in each time and told me to leave them alone "or else." Of course, I had to test her to see what "or else" meant. To my dismay, Grandma inflicted the ultimate punishment on me—a massive kissing attack that left my face wet and smelling like honeysuckle, her perfume. I don't think I bothered the girls after that. (At least not for the rest of that day.)

The other side of the family found Grandma Helen, giver of quirky gifts. Since she and Grandpa George were both schoolteachers, we could count on getting something educational. Once I got a book about ancient Egyptian artifacts, and another time a book called *The History of Ships*. Then there was the tantalizing life account of Fernando Ortega the Explorer—*without illustrations*.

I really wanted to say, "Grandma, you missed a perfectly good opportunity to give me something great." Instead, I exchanged a knowing look with my sisters. At least we were in it together. I'd turn and attempt to be genuine. "I love it, Grandma!" I'd say, in one of my finest acting performances. (Where was the Emmy-nominating committee then?) Grandma Jeanne always gave a card with money in it. Now *that* was a gift I could take to the bank.

Grandma Helen kept a very proper house. We had nametags at our places for holiday meals above the fancy china. Ketchup was forbidden at the table because it "destroyed" her perfectly good food. You couldn't have a glass of water until you were halfway through dinner because if you filled up on water, you couldn't eat the food.

Who fills up on water?

We much preferred the more casual dining experiences at my other grandparents'. But boy, did Grandma Helen make the most amazing four-layer Ghirardelli chocolate cake. We'd rather she made us that cake than get another book on *Thomas Edison: The Teen Years.*

Grandpa George was a gymnast and had a set of great big rings on two long ropes hanging over the trampoline buried in the yard. (The top of it was at ground level.) He also tied a thick rope with knots in it. We'd grab that rope and climb to the top of the jungle gym to swing down like Tarzan on a vine. And he had a special talent: He could make delicious, rich fudge from scratch.

My mom's parents were lots of fun. Grandma Jeanne helped me conspire against the girls and made great dinners where ketchup was welcomed. Grandpa Frank was the quintessential grandfather. He sat us on his knee and told stories. He had a big belly—possibly full of jelly—that made him perfect to dress as Santa at Christmas time.

Uncle Frankie

Uncle Frankie was the best big brother I never had. He was my hero. My mom's baby brother was only seven years older than me, so we got into a lot of trouble together and loved every minute of it.

He didn't mind hanging out with a little guy. He let me run as fast as I could through my grandparents' hallways and slam into him, holding couch pillows to cushion the blows. We spent hours making 10-foot-long gum wrapper chains for no reason. For our Hot Wheels, we made our own tracks with paper, folding up the edges, creating curves and supports for bridges. One time we went on a hike in the woods, and when we were three hours late coming home, my parents panicked and called the cops to come find us.

The thing we both liked to do best was to go lizard hunting. He'd take me to the dry creek bed in Fillmore where lizards basked in the sun on the small rocks. We snuck up on them, throwing our shirts on top of them. They responded by skittering under the rock. We'd wrap the shirt around both the lizard and rock and scoop them from their hiding place.

Frankie had a shirt that had the image of a ruler on it, so we held the lizards up to see how long they were. Then we perched the lizards on our shoulders for a ride while we hiked. If they lasted long enough to make it home, we kept them and fed them tiny grub.

Later, someone showed me how to make a lizard noose and it revolutionized lizard hunting. It was so easy, all the fun was zapped from it.

At Home

My parents had a traditional marriage—almost. Until I got into the business, Mom took care of the home and Dad taught at a junior high school. Dad was always the leader of the family—there was never any doubt about that. He got home at 3:00 P.M. each day, which allowed him the freedom to help Mom clean, prepare dinner and do the dishes.

Dad ran a tight ship with a firm hand. On weekdays, we had to be up at 6:15 in order to eat the healthy breakfast he had cooked for us. If you wanted to eat, you had to be done digesting your food by 6:40 or you missed your chance. Five minutes later, we took turns washing the dishes so we could be out the door at 7:05.

On his way to work, Dad drove us to school in this really ugly red VW truck. In junior high, I asked him to drop me off at the corner so that I could walk the rest of the way. Dad was no dummy. He knew I was embarrassed, so he circled the block and came around just in time to yell: "Hey, son! Have a good day at school. Daddy loves ya!"

Dad's love extended to applying corporal punishment when we disobeyed. He took off his belt, folded it in half, snapped it together and said in a loud voice, "The long arm of the law reaches out!" I'd run to my bedroom and stuff books, shirts or underwear down my pants, hoping he wouldn't notice that his son had developed extra junk in the trunk.

The real maddening thing I learned later was that when Dad was supposedly punishing Candace, he'd go in there, snapping his belt. But when the door closed behind him, he'd slap the belt on the bed while Candace yelped like she'd gotten spanked. You never saw a performance like that from her on *Full House*.

One day when I felt Dad was being a jerk, I got fed up and mad. I had no idea what made him so cranky this time. He was on us for nothing we could figure out. I gathered my sisters and the Rock boys and set them to work.

A week or so before, we had all helped Dad picket a man's business who had not done the work in our house as promised. I saw how well that worked, so I found some wood slats in the garage and stapled pieces of notebook paper to them. On the papers I wrote in bubble letters:

DAD'S A LEAN, MEAN, SCREAMIN' MACHINE.
DAD'S ON THE WARPATH AGAIN.

And an acrostic of his name, Robert: Rat, Ostrich legs, Bird legs . . . (sadly, no one can remember the rest).

We were ready for him when he got home from work: He pulled in the driveway to find us circling the yard, chanting the slogans we had written on the signs. All he could do was laugh. He laughed so hard that the pictures he took of us were cockeyed and cut off. But the scheme worked—Dad lightened up.

We used to watch my favorite show, *Happy Days*, after dinner as a family, but we never went to bed like ordinary kids. Dad loved affecting a voice from his barrel of bad accents. Instead of being told it was time for bed, Dad broke into song: "Happy trails to you, until we meet again!" or "The party's over . . . let's call it a day!" To this day, my sisters and I hate those songs, in part because we knew that the party *wasn't* over. It was just beginning—without us. Once we were in bed, the Rocks would come over with (appropriately enough) Rocky Road ice cream for the adults to share. *So* not fair.

Mom tried her hand at business when we were little. She taught macramé classes in our garage and made enough money for my parents to splurge on a family buffet at a sit-down restaurant once in a while. But she invested most of her time and energy into loving and caring for us kids. I remember Mom singing or humming while she did the household chores. I admired her from my earliest memories—but, like most kids, wouldn't have admitted it on paper.

Mom and I wrestled all the time. You'd think I would have won those fights, but she usually did. The Bausmith girls were all hearty and strong. My Aunt Joanne was a body builder and the first woman on the Los Angeles Fire Department. These were no helpless maidens. Dad often had to intervene, "Careful, Barbara! Don't hurt him! Watch the face! Don't hurt the face!"

Together we did calisthenics at rest stops on long road trips. Dad, whistle in mouth, marked how many jumping jacks or pushups we could muster.

Mom and Dad encouraged us to get involved in anything that interested us. Mom was the taxi driver, schlepping us around town to this lesson or that practice. I played soccer and baseball and rode motocross. As I grew older I added racquetball, skiing, hiking, camping—anything active and outdoorsy. I also loved indoor activities that required precision and concentration, like putting together plastic models of Corvettes and Mustangs. I even put together a model of the human body.

Sisters

To make my childhood even more traditional, I had three little sisters to tease mercilessly. I pinned their arms down with my knees and tried to dangle a long string of spit close to their screaming mouth without it actually falling in. (I didn't always succeed.) I rubbed my thumb and forefinger behind their ear to make them think a bug had chosen their ear as a new home. I scooted up the walls of our darkened, narrow hallway—back against one wall, feet against the other—and perched against the ceiling for a few minutes. Then I called one of my sisters and when she came through the hallway, I pounced and flattened her.

One day Melissa and Bridgette were swimming in the pool next door. With one of the frozen chickens I kept to feed my snakes, I sat on the other side of the wall and calculated where it needed to go. I yelled, "Bridgette! Melissa! Look out!" I made chicken noises—"Baccch, baccch, baccch baach." The next thing they saw was a frozen chicken flying over the wall, landing in the pool. It made a satisfying splash and an even more satisfying reaction.

I suppose one of the meanest things (not *the* meanest—that comes later) I did to my sister was when Melissa and I had to go to the doctor for something, probably to get blood drawn. All the way there I whispered, "Melissa, this is going to hurt *so* bad. It's going to hurt more than anything you've ever had done before."

At the doctor's office I continued to harass her. "It's gonna hurt so much, you're gonna scream for your life."

By the time the nurse ushered her into the room, she was sobbing. But the tables turned and Melissa took the shot like a trooper. I, however, got one look at that needle in my arm and it was *my* turn to start sobbing like a schoolgirl who had just lost her pack of markers.

Mom made sure I spent a lot of time in my room "contemplating" how mean I was to my sisters.

I don't suppose it should come as any surprise that Bridgette found the perfect chance to play by my rules.

We lived on a great street with a bit of an incline. The kids played in the street and cars patiently navigated around us. We built ramps and jumps for our skateboards and bikes. One day, I got the great idea to have Bridgette pedal her bike really fast and pull me on a rope while I rode on my skateboard—I figured I could get more speed with her pulling me than I could get on my own.

"Bridge," I said, "you have to promise me one thing."

"What?"

"Don't go off the jump."

She scrunched her face and said, "I wasn't going to."

"You've got to promise me."

"Don't worry about it, Kirk."

"Bridge—promise me!"

With her sworn vow, we walked to the top of the street. I gave Bridgette The Look. She straddled her bike and looked back at me, making sure I had the rope in hand.

"Don't, Bridgette. Whatever you do, do *not* go off the jump."

She waved me away and took off pedaling as fast as her legs would pump. To this day, I don't know why I didn't let go of that rope. I *do* know why Bridgette veered away at the last moment. I, on the other hand, flew over the ramp and into the air.

Fortunately, the concrete broke my fall.

Lying in the street, I nearly blacked out from the pain. Bridgette ran into the house screaming, "Mom! Mom! Kirk somehow got hurt!"

Mom took one look and hoisted me into the car. En route to the emergency room, Bridgette's face appeared over the back seat. To rub it in, I asked in a pitiful voice, "Mom, am I gonna die?"

As much fun as it would have been to torture my sister by dying, I only broke the radius and the ulna bones in my wrist.

All Boy

I've always had the ability to memorize complicated things and remember them. I mastered the Rubik's Cube by reading a book on it and memorizing the patterns and methods of aligning the colors quickly. I entered a contest at Magic Mountain theme park with a hundred other kids. I did it in 60 seconds, but the kid who won did it in 23.

Same for the video games I played. I read a book on how to master Pac-Man. The book had drawings of the patterns he could take in the maze. There were dozens of boards to memorize, but once I did, I could play the game for hours on a single quarter at Chuck E. Cheese.

Skee Ball had the added draw of spitting out tickets when you scored points that could be used to buy all kinds of stuff. Because my friends and I were more interested in the stuff than the game, we'd trick little kids: One of us distracted the kid while the other put a foot on the strip of tickets to snap them off without the kid realizing it. We didn't have any problem using these stolen tickets to buy the stuff we wanted.

One day my dad found out and put all the stolen tickets in the trashcan. There were hundreds of them. We dug through the garbage until we found them, all soaking wet. We put them in paper towels in the microwave to dry them out, which only scorched 'em (giving new meaning to the term "hot goods").

Holidays

Mom and Dad enjoyed going out of their way to make every holiday special. Even non-holidays could be celebrated. They were always up for a party. For our birthdays, we could invite friends over from school. (When I blew out my birthday candles and made a wish, I wished for two things—that one day I would meet a beautiful girl to marry and that I'd never get cancer. I'm 2 for 2, so far.)

Like Easter and birthdays, Christmas was a big deal in our family. Grandma Jeanne had the best tree in the world. It snowed little Styrofoam balls that fell around the tree into a trough underneath. Something sucked those tiny balls up through the tree so they could get out the top, snowing once again.

I tried to stay up as late as I could to catch Santa Claus, and never did. In the morning we all had to wait in our rooms until we got the go-ahead. When the signal came, we tore through the living room into the den to find a sea of presents. We were gluttonous little creatures. Sometimes our parents made us put the presents in piles and take turns one by one. It forced us to share in each others' joy, but secretly we couldn't care less what anyone else got.

The day ended with a Christmas dinner big enough to feed an army. We almost always had people with us at dinner who had no one to spend the holiday with. They could be nearly strangers, but Mom and Dad opened our home to them.

We didn't have a nativity, nor did we tell the Christmas story. I knew that in religious homes, Jesus had something to do with Christmas, but wasn't sure how He was connected to it. Was He a special carpenter in Santa's village?

One year I got a BB gun as a gift. I practiced shooting soda cans and empty furniture boxes, but that got boring. I decided I needed to try my skills on a moving target. I'm sorry to say, I shot the neighbor's cat in the leg. The vet bill came and my BB gun went.

I know, I know . . . I claim I always wanted to do the best thing, the right thing. But sometimes that excluded the insanity of being all boy.

Note

1. Barbara Cameron with Lissa Halls Johnson, *A Full House of Growing Pains* (Alachua, FL: Bridge-Logos Publishers, 2006), p. 7.

Chapter 4

The Great and Terrible Agent

1979

Around the dinner table one night Mom asked, "Hey, guys, remember your friend Adam Rich? He's on a TV show. I thought we'd go to the lady who helps him and see if she would help you get on television, too. Would you like that?"

Mom's eager face suggested only one correct response: "Yeah!"

Adam was the son of my mom's friend Fran, a former New Yorker who liked to wear nightgowns and smelled of smoke. Mom had shown Fran a photo of us kids dressed to the nines at our aunt's wedding. Her son, Adam, had recently become a child star as Nicholas Bradford on *Eight Is Enough* and she now insisted that Mom consider us for commercials. "They'd be perfect!" she persisted.

Though at first she resisted, Mom let Fran show the photo of us to Adam's agent, Iris Burton, who was the top children's agent in town. Shockingly, Iris agreed to see us.

We're Off to See the Wizard

Mom called me into the bathroom last, after making my sisters look really girly. "Kirk," she said as she brushed my hair and straightened my shirt and jeans, "I want you to be nice to your sisters. No pranks today, okay?" There was an edge to her voice that meant business.

I nodded.

I wanted to trip Bridgette as she ran down the hall, but I practiced restraint. I wanted to thump the girls on their heads as they got into the

VW, but I resisted the nagging urge. I wanted to poke Candace until she swatted me, but today I knew better.

As we drove down the freeway in our VW bus, I sat next to the window and stared out, trying to be a good kid. My parents stared straight ahead for a long time, not saying a word. I knew this must be serious business.

Mom read from a map and pointed at street signs while Dad drove on winding roads to an exclusive neighborhood in Hollywood Hills. She tapped the window. "There it is, Robert."

Dad gave a low whistle and pulled into the driveway of a house. "Bet this gal doesn't re-use dryer sheets," he quipped.

I don't remember much except it was a *big* house. I guess I was expecting to go to an office building somewhere, but this woman's office was in that big house.

Mom seemed very nervous. "Be on your best behavior," she said, popping open her door.

Dad turned around and said in his stern voice, "You know how to behave. If you're good, we'll stop by McDonald's for an ice cream on the way home." Dad might be strict. But one thing was for sure: Whatever he said, he meant. We four kids looked at each other, making it clear with arched eyebrows and glares that no one was to mess up our chance for ice cream.

Silent as church mice, we exited in single file, trudged up the driveway and followed the sidewalk to the back of the house. A woman and her daughter emerged through a pair of French doors. She gave a smile that seemed forced and Mom motioned for us to go inside.

Inside, the office was even more intimidating. Black-and-white glossies of famous child stars filled the walls. Bridgette saw Adam's picture, elbowed me and pointed. I nodded, scanning the other photos.

In the back of the room behind a cloud of smoke sat an old Jewish woman, beckoning with what must have been a long, bony finger, her raspy voice saying, "Come in, come in." She looked like Larry King in drag, speaking in a smoke-scarred voice, "How are ya?" She motioned toward a sofa and some chairs. "Have a seat."

We obeyed in unison.

Mom could barely speak, so Dad tried to get a little bit of conversation going. We were all terrified of this gruff, powerful woman. She was the most prestigious agent in town. The best. And though at nine I wasn't sure what an "agent" was, I knew she must be extremely important to make even my parents nervous. Besides, I was afraid of anyone I didn't know, let alone someone hiding behind a shroud of smoke. My imagination began to get the best of me.

It was like we were in the presence of the Wizard. Instead of "I am the Great and Terrible Oz," she was the Great and Terrible Agent.

"You," she said, pointing at me with a demanding finger. "Stand."

Being on my best behavior meant I obeyed authority—immediately. I popped off that sofa without a split second of hesitation.

She got up from behind her desk and moved to the side, cigarette dangling from the corner of her mouth. My heart bumped around in my chest. She walked around, eyeballing me up and down. She peered at my hair and grunted, "You wanna be an actor?"

I watched her cigarette bounce up and down as she spoke. I tried not to think about how Dad and Mom always told us that smoking would kill us. *Focus, Kirk, focus.*

I nodded my answer. I must have. I wouldn't dare move an inch unless she told me to do so.

Iris took a long drag and studied me a bit more. "Well, say this for me: 'Hey, Mom, I wanna go to McDonalds.' "

I repeated her words in an unemotional, parroting way, "Hey, Mom, I wanna go to McDonalds."

"No, no, no! You have to say it like you really wanna go to McDonalds. Say it with energy."

"Hey, Mom! I wanna go to McDonalds!" I said with enthusiasm.

"Now try, 'Hey, Tony, those Kellogg's Frosted Flakes taste gggrr-eeeaaatt!' "

In my very best monotone I said, "Hey, Tony, those Kellogg's Frosted Flakes taste good."

"No, no. They taste grrreeaat!"

"They taste greeeaattt!" I added pizzazz and a smile and hoped that was okay.

"Look at those Hot Wheels go!" she said.

This time I knew I was supposed to be excited, so I pretended I was saying it to Uncle Frankie.

"All right. Sit. You," she motioned to Bridgette. "Stand."

The Great and Terrible Agent went down the line asking us all the same questions, looking at all of us the same way—like the type of jungle cat that eats her young. When she finished her perfunctory interviews, she looked at Mom and Dad, pointed to us and said, "I'll give him a try for a year." She skipped Bridgette and pointed to Melissa, "I'll take her. Bring the little one back in a year; she's too young."

"What about Bridgette?" Mom asked, surprised.

"Nope," Iris said in her blunt way.

"Why?"

Iris didn't answer Mom. We had all thought she would take Bridgette, the one always performing at home, singing and dancing like a woodland creature in her own private Disney flick. Every photo we had of Bridgette featured the biggest smile—one that made her nose and eyes disappear into her cheeks.

"I'll need headshots," she barked, as though we knew what she meant. "Black-and-white glossies."

"Can I take them?" Mom asked.

Iris exhaled. "Sure."

Inside the car, Bridgette leaned between the seats and asked Mom, "Why didn't she want me? Why didn't she pick me?"

I played with the seatbelt as Mom tried to answer a question she didn't have the answer to. I secretly wished that Iris lady *had* picked Bridgette instead of me. Life would have been simpler for me. But how could I tell my mom? She looked so excited.

But these fears were eclipsed once we pulled into the drive-thru. Everything changes under the glow of the golden arches.

Audition Land

It wasn't too many days later when Mom got her first call from Iris Burton telling her the location of my first audition. "Kirk!" she said the moment I dropped my book bag on the floor. "You're going on your first acting try-out!" (She hadn't yet learned the lingo.)

I had no idea what that meant, but I was quickly carted off to Adam Rich's hair stylist upon the insistence of Fran. It seemed exciting, driving to the studio the first time. Would we get lost? Would we make it on time? Would the studio lot be cool? I was living in my own reality show montage—I just needed a rap song to underscore the drama.

We made it on time, and it *was* fascinating—but not in the way we expected. The building looked a lot like any old office building. We walked down a long hallway that looked pretty much like any hallway—scuffed walls, bad neon lighting, chipped ceiling tiles. Whether Mom chatted the whole way or was quiet, I don't remember. I'm sure I didn't say anything.

"Here it is," she said, a little breathless. She turned the knob and opened the door.

Fran had told her what to expect, so she headed toward a counter that had a sign-in sheet and a stack of photocopied scripts (called "sides"). I followed her, feeling every eye on me. I didn't like that. I didn't want people looking at me, but they quickly turned back to their conversations.

The weird thing is that all the kids looked just like me: curly-haired Caucasians in dork-tastic clothes. I don't know if Mom noticed. She was busy filling out the sign-in sheet.

We didn't have headshots yet, so Mom handed the lady a Polaroid she'd taken of me in front of the house. She had written "Kirk Cameron, Age 10, Iris Burton Agency" on it and stapled it to my résumé—which probably should just have listed *playing, eating* and *torturing* as the skills I'd mastered thus far.

Mom took a copy of the sides and said, "Look, hon . . . this is for a chili commercial." She scanned the room and led me to a couple of vacant chairs. "Let's practice!" she said at a volume I'm sure everyone heard.

"This chili is better than my mom makes!" Mom said, cheesily.

I looked at her like she was nuts, because she was—especially if she thought I would say the line like that. "This chili is better than my mom makes," I repeated.

"No, Kirk, be happier."

She said the line again. I noticed other moms doing the same thing, until the door opened and a new mother-son combination walked in. It didn't take long to see the games the other mothers played. It was a catty battle of "My kid is better than yours." Even at nine, it was incredibly obvious.

Over the next 40 minutes, I watched the door open at least six times. All the moms did the same thing: When they signed their kid in, they paused at the sign-in sheet to scan the names above theirs. I later discovered they were trying to see which kid had which agent. Everyone knew the top agencies. And if Iris Burton represented a kid, everyone knew the competition.

If a recognizable kid walked in, you could almost hear the groans: "Oh, great. River Phoenix is here." We quickly learned it didn't take long to predict who would get the jobs.

When the mothers talked to each other, they spoke ridiculously loud so that the rest of the room could hear. "Oh, yes," one would say in faux-humility, "*My* son just got off the set of a Richard *Donner* film. He only had three lines, but we're hearing a lot of early buzz."

"Well, it's not hard to see why," the other would reply, not meaning a word of it.

"I'm sure it's just a matter of time for your little guy," the first would say with utmost insincerity.

Some moms used the phone on the counter to call their child's agent, speaking loudly if there was good news. "Oh, he needs to be at *Disney* tomorrow at one? Of course, we can be there. With bells on. . . . Oh, in overalls? No, 'bells on' is just an expression. Of course he can wear overalls. It's a movie about a dairy farm." Mom looked at me and rolled her eyes. I smiled back.

These kinds of incidents gave us an understanding of what was meant by the term "stage mother." A stage mom was generally someone from the Valley who tried to look like she was from Beverly Hills, living her dreams vicariously through her offspring. They were always made up, artificial, loud and pretentious.

A few auditions in, Mom and I learned to find a private corner or hallway to practice. She loved to coach me on my delivery, but I didn't like her giving me suggestions. I started to think about the words on the page and what the commercial was trying to sell. I learned to go to a quiet, internal place where I could hear my own voice saying it. I tried to give the casting directors what they wanted to hear, what sounded best. Watching TV in the evenings became my research.

If the line was, "Make your reservations today," I would try different inflections.

"*Make* your reservations today."

"Make *your* reservations today."

"Make your *reservations* today."

"Make your reservations *today*."

Usually I felt the right way to say the line in my gut. The only time I performed it out loud was when the camera rolled. I don't know if that reluctance was a self-conscious thing or a deliberate attempt to keep the line from getting stale by saying it too much.

The casting director always said something like, "Thanks, that was really good," but I was very hard on myself. *That was awful, I'm really terrible at this*, I regularly thought to myself.

Some kids spend years going to auditions and don't land more than a commercial or two, so it was surprising that my sixth audition was my launching pad.

Behind the Curtain

Moms were not allowed behind the audition door, but they often leaned next to it to eavesdrop. If the kid inside was known for booking a lot of commercials, many of the other stage moms leaned toward the door, looking as though a stiff wind had blown through the room.

For commercial auditions, I stood directly over a piece of tape on the floor, looking at the camera. At "Go," I said, "Hi, my name is Kirk Cameron. I am 10 years old and I'm with the Iris Burton Agency." I tried to sound bright and full of life, but not fake or over the top—just to let them see the happier side of my personality.

The casting director's job is to get kids on tape to send to the producer or director. Often, that was the only person I could distinguish in the darkened corner, though I could see several others. Their silhouettes were imposing.

"Okay, Kirk. We'd like you to add just a hint of sadness to your voice," the casting director said. "Pretend your dog died."

"Say it with a British accent this time."

"Now say the line like a young Brazilian street boy trying to sell enough cashews to pay for his own education."

No matter how challenging their direction, I did my best to please.

On my sixth audition I suddenly felt terribly shy. The waiting room insanity had gotten to me.

Instead of calling us in privately, the casting director brought us into the room by groups of four. They lined us up and we each gave our name and information before spitting out the scripted line. As each boy spoke, one after the other, I got more and more nervous.

When it was my turn I was so embarrassed standing in front of these other people, so afraid that I wouldn't do a good job, that I turned my back to the camera and started to cry. All I could think was, *I can't do this.*

Mom remembers that they sent all the other kids out and then the casting director took me aside to play catch for a few moments before giving me the opportunity to try again.

I did it without a problem and got my first callback. (The studios always have at least one callback so the people who weren't there during the first round can see how the kids perform a second or third time.) Then one afternoon I was sitting at our table doing homework when Mom answered the phone. She sounded like she was excited and trying not to be. She hung up and came running over to me. "Ooohhh, honey! You got it, you got it!"

I tried to pretend I was excited, too—but I really didn't know what I was in for.

My First Commercial

Though auditions had become an ordinary part of life, being on a set was all very new. Mom and I were tentative about where to go, where to sit, what to say, who to talk to. But it was so exciting and the crew bent over backward for the actors—even kid actors. I thought this was really strange, because I was accustomed to sitting at the little kids' table of life. Someone explained that the commercial couldn't be made without the actors. They were the ones who were selling the product for the sponsor. The crew kept an upbeat attitude so the actors would be more relaxed and more likely to do a good job.

Bonnie, the casting director, helped a lot. She came to greet us as soon as she saw us wandering around, lost and confused.

"Kirk!" she said, reaching to shake my hand. "It's so nice to see you again." She then reached for my mother's hand. "You must be Mom. I'm Bonnie."

"Barbara," Mom said, looking almost as excited as I was.

Since the shoot was in Griffith Park, the area had trucks and cables scattered everywhere.

"Follow me," Bonnie said. "I'll take you to the Honeywagon."

"Uh," I said, "I thought this was a commercial for Count Chocula, not honey."

Bonnie smiled. "That's what we call the dressing room trailer."

She took us to a trailer big enough to require towing by a semi. It had stalls along the length of it. I stared in awe at the doors, each one with a name on it. Mom took a picture with me standing next to my name, even though it was only written in black marker on masking tape. I felt very important and was both eager and frightened for the real thing to begin.

"You can leave your things in here. It's yours for the next two days."

The dressing room had a bench seat on one wall. Across from that was a desk with a well-lit mirror, a place where I could hang my clothes, and a bathroom.

"I'll show you how to find Craft Services now," Bonnie said. I wondered why there would be a table for arts and crafts on a movie set. Weren't we here to act?

I quickly caught on to the lingo. Craft Services was the food area spread out beneath a huge California oak tree. Bagels, donuts, rolls, croissants, loaves of white and wheat bread, a variety of muffins and sweet rolls—it was carb heaven. Topping that was the table of endless candy, as if the world's finest trick-or-treater had been robbed. "It's free, have whatever you want," Bonnie shrugged.

I couldn't believe it. I snagged a bagel and smeared it with cream cheese. It was my first of many, many years of free bagels. (To this day I won't pay for bagels or cream cheese—not when I can score them for free on film sets.)

"We'll start you in school first, Kirk," Bonnie said, beckoning me to follow her to a table underneath another oak tree. Starting my day with school interfered with my crack at the candy table, but at least it would be a shortened day of education. This commercial shoot was going to keep me legitimately out of school for *two days*, quite the adventure! California law required only three hours a day with the tutor. Mom had gotten homework assignments from my real schoolteachers for them to use.

"Hi, Kirk, I'm Pamela. I'll be your teacher for today. What grade are you in?"

Pamela was responsible for more than making sure I got my papers done. She had the responsibility of protecting me on the set, making sure the studios were following child labor laws.

"Why don't you begin with this math? I'll be right here if you have any questions," she said.

Not much later, a man came to get me. "We're all set up for you, Kirk. Ready?"

I nodded, my eyes like saucers with anticipation. The saucers got even bigger when I saw the Panavision cameras with the big black lenses, giant wheels of film tape behind, each one resting on dolly tracks. I followed the man through a flurry of activity, fascinated with the 50 people running around moving cables and lights. The sound guy held a boom mike with a gray furry cover that resembled a dead possum.

I had been told they would use stand-ins to do my part while I was in school, so the crew could determine the light and camera positions. It was very strange to see an adult about my height and coloring—he wasn't a kid; he was a Little Person. I found out later they used Little People a lot because, as adults, they could work long adult hours. At least I now knew what my face would look like with a five o'clock shadow.

For the rest of the day the same things repeated over and over. I did a take until the director said, "Cut." When adjustments were going to take longer than 20 minutes, they brought the Little Person back in and he took my place while I went back to school.

By the end of the day, I was hooked. *This was great!* I wanted to do more of it. I thought I must be pretty hot stuff to be getting all that red carpet treatment—my own private teacher, a dressing room, endless candy. And all the people were falling all over themselves for me. It was a huge ego boost.

After we gathered my things and fell into the car, exhausted, I turned to Mom and said, "Can we do this again?"

She smiled and tousled my hair. "Sure, Kirk."

Becoming a Pro

After Count Chocula I felt I could do this well. I quickly became more confident in my auditions. I received callbacks most of the time, booking a commercial every third or fourth interview, resulting in a total of 30 or 40 commercials throughout my early acting years. My sister Melissa auditioned off and on for years, and though she was very talented, she landed only one commercial and a few series pilots. (She eventually quit because she hated to be on camera.) I knew some kids went on auditions for years and never got a job.

> I didn't even know for quite some time how well Kirk was doing until Barb told me some camera guys had said, "He's got something going with the camera." I thought, *What are you talking about?*
>
> Robert Cameron, Kirk's dad

I don't know what I did differently than other kids, but it always seemed to go well with me inside the audition room.

In spite of all the jobs I landed, I never got used to auditions. I hated the entire process.

When I got a message in class that Mom was there to get me or when I saw the VW bug waiting outside in the pick-up lane, I thought, *Oh, no, I hate this. I don't want to do it anymore. Why can't I be like every other kid and stay in school, or go home to play with my friends?* I slowed my pace, slumped my shoulders and dropped my head. Everything about me sagged, making me resemble a thin, scrappy Eeyore.

Mom was always chipper, attempting to zap some life into me. "Hi, honey! How was your school day?"

I either shrugged or grunted. I didn't want to talk to her.

"Why don't we stop at McDonald's? We'll get you some ice cream, or a Happy Meal with a toy inside. Whatever you want."

"Mooooom, I'm too old to care about toys," I'd whine. A few moments went by. "What do you think the toy is?"

She didn't fool me. I knew she was trying to cheer me up. I accepted the food and the toy, but I held on to my bad mood like a winter cold. I liked being a grump and had no desire to snap out of it. I didn't want to give in.

And I *really* didn't want to put on the stupid, ugly clothes she always brought. She learned very early that kids who are the most successful in auditions had the same look all the time. They had to look like their head shots. And if it was a callback, they needed to look exactly as they did in the first audition. So every time I auditioned I had to wear the same dorky outfit. It became my uniform. I cannot express how much I loathed that red-and-tan striped IZOD sitting on a hanger in the rear window just waiting to be put on and *tucked inside* my jeans. Was there anything worse?

Oh, yes.

Not only did I have to tuck that shirt into a pair of stiff Toughskin jeans, I had to cinch the whole thing with a belt. And then when we got to the studio, Mom whipped out her brush and started in on my bowl-cut hair, brushing it to be smooth and stick straight. "Come on, Mom," I'd protest. "I'm 10!"

"Oh, stop it. Your friends aren't even here."

She had a point. Still, I didn't want the security guard, the janitor or even the Arrowhead water delivery guy seeing my hair brushed by my mother.

We went into the audition building and immediately started rehearsing lines. Mom was always so eager, and that drove me nuts. "Let's practice the lines. You do this part and I'll do that," she'd chirp. When I didn't go for it, she'd say, "Okay, sweetheart, after the audition, where would you like to go to lunch?"

I'd heave a big sigh and say, "McDonald's. I've been thinking about a Big Mac all day."

I never told her, but I was self-conscious about practicing with her. I was afraid that she would make fun of me, or that I'd get it wrong in her eyes. Either of those would make it harder for me to deliver the line on camera.

I dreaded auditions where I had to sing. There was no advance warning about these musical commercials. I stepped through the magic door and after I said my line, the director, shrouded in black, called out, "Hey. We'd like you to sing something. Pick whatever you want."

Great.

So there in front of a camera I'd have to come up with some little ditty on my own, or they might ask me to sing "Happy Birthday." I hated it.

The other tough thing was if I had to cry on cue. Commercials didn't generally call for crying, but often auditions for movies and TV shows did. Those were very uncomfortable. How can you cry with all those people looking at you? I'm sure that, somewhere on the other side of town, Tracey Gold had no problem with it. But I hated tearing up for strangers.

As the years went on, things got worse. Or rather, *I* got worse. I learned that the cure for the boredom and depression of having to audition was to fall asleep quickly. That was also my way of getting back at Mom because I knew she wanted to talk. I put my head back on that seat and went right to sleep. An hour later, just as Mom was parking, I'd wake up, stretch and get out of the car—all without talking to her.

As I walked into the audition room I was so groggy. She'd look at me and say, "Do you even want to do this?"

I shrugged a wordless answer. I didn't have the courage to tell my mom I didn't want to go anymore. My parents had always said, "You don't look like you're enjoying this. If you don't want to do this, just tell us. You can leave at any time."

"No, it's okay," I'd say and slip away to hide out in my bedroom.

I didn't feel like Mom was forcing me to continue. I simply didn't have the nerve to stop. It's like a kid in gymnastics who's doing really well and everyone is telling him, "You've got a gift. You've got talent." And when he's there, he does a good job and it feels good. It's complicated—half of him wants to continue and half wants to quit.

Mom only saw the grumpy, groggy kid in the waiting room. What she didn't know was that I knew I could turn on the exact personality I needed, perking up the moment I went through the magic door to the audition room. In some ways, I wanted her to think I was blowing it miserably in there.

I never showed Mom that part of me. I knew what she wanted—and I was determined not to give it to her. I knew she wanted me to talk to her. I knew she wanted me to show her what I was going to do. I knew she wanted to know the reaction of the casting director. She was always so anxious after it was over: "So? How did it go? What'd they say?"

Most of the time I didn't even look at her. Occasionally I threw her a bone and say flatly, "I dunno. They said, 'Thanks, fine, good.'"

Sometimes I put on the shy act instead. It was my way of selfishly doing what I wanted and showing my parents I was in charge by not talking—exactly what some married couples do. *If I don't talk, then I win. I've got the power!*

What a jerk! Why did I do that? I think it was partly a way of punishing her for taking me away from my friends. Partly it was a control thing. It was my way of being in charge, of being the boss. *I can do what I want*, it silently conveyed. What could she do to me?

I was so awful to her, yet I don't remember her ever getting frustrated with me. She tirelessly drove me an hour each way—sometimes longer in traffic—and waited hours for me to finish. I was so unappreciative of all she did.

Eventually Mom gave up trying to get me to rehearse with her. She says that one day after a Universal Studios audition when I flatly refused to say a line her way, she came to the conclusion, *Okay, he's obviously doing something right. He doesn't need my help anymore. He's booking the jobs and I can simply be the chaperone.* She quietly continued her taxi service for this little selfish brat.

If Mom had called me on my attitude and said, "You know what? You're being a jerk. And you're being disrespectful to me. We're going home. We're not doing this anymore," that probably would have gotten me off my high horse. I would have jumped off that horse and apologized. Because I really *loved* the work—and deep down, I loved my mom.

Branching Out

Work never failed to give me that same ego boost I had experienced when filming that first cereal commercial. People bent over backward to give me what I wanted. And what kid doesn't want adults eating out of his hand, catering to his every wish? Because life was all about getting to the place where *I* could be happy all the time, acting was the perfect venue.

It wasn't only the ego boost that kept me going. I truly *loved* what I did. When it came time for me to perform, I did the job. It helped that I was good with memorization and knew how to give the crew what they needed. I got a lot of praise for that.

Mom received kudos as well. They'd tell her, "Your son is such a great kid," blah, blah, blah. That made my mom feel good about herself. Besides, being on the set was fascinating to her.

I was incredibly fortunate that the commercials began to come fast and frequent. Now *I* was the kid that caused moms to whisper, "Look. Kirk Cameron is here," and to be discouraged, figuring (falsely) that because I booked a lot of commercials, I was a shoo-in for every audition. (Though I did book a good number.)

I started to recognize other kids from the auditions. River Phoenix was one of the regulars at that time. He was one of Iris Burton's big hits. We would often audition for the same parts. Sadly, he later died of a drug overdose outside the Viper Room in Hollywood.

I did commercials for Count Chocula, Polaroid, McDonald's, Formula 409, He-Man, Kool-Aid, Pepsi, Fruit Roll-Ups, All laundry detergent, Hawaiian Punch, Northwest Orient Airlines—and so many more that none of us can remember all the products I represented.

I did a commercial for EuroDisney, filmed in California's Disneyland. I had to take on an accent and pretend to be a little English kid, in a whole different country with a whole different family. They set this big ice cream sundae in front of me and I had to say, "Cor, Dad, what a big ice cream!" Not only was I at Disneyland, I had all this ice cream to dive into at every take.

They shot the commercial on Employee Appreciation Day, so the park was shut down to the public and only the employees and their families were there. When they finished filming the commercial, I got to wander around a nearly empty Disneyland and go on any ride I wished. And because there were no lines, I simply walked to the front and got on the ride, going on as many times as I wanted to.

In the arcade, an employee followed me around and put a key in the machine of any game I wanted to play.

"Ding! Ding! Ding!" the machine responded and I magically had 30 credits to play that game or any others. It was a dream come true.

Probably the most fun I ever had doing a commercial was for Wrigley's gum. Once they shouted, "Action!" a group of kids piled into a river raft and we shot down the white-water rapids of the Kern River. We had to do it about a half-dozen times to be sure they had great shots. Awesome.

It wasn't too shabby that I got paid very well for all this "work" on rapids and in theme parks. In the '80s, the going rate was 5 to 10 grand for two days of commercial work.

I also enjoyed the part of my imagination that commercials brought to life. For two days, I belonged to a whole new family living in a different reality. That girl was my sister. That kid, my brother. It was fun to pretend that these other people were my parents. "Hey, Dad!" I'd say to some strange guy who was my actor parent. I threw myself into it, wondering what life would be like if these people were truly my mom and dad.

When I was 11, I landed the part of Liam in a TV movie called *Goliath Awaits*, starring Eddie Albert. The movie was about people living on a partially sunken ship. It wasn't until after I booked it that they told me the part required scuba diving. Since I'd never done that, I had to take lessons. The studio sent an instructor to our house with scuba gear. Our neighbors across the street let us use their pool.

The training didn't help a lot. Although I only had to swim around under the surface with the tank on my back, I couldn't get myself to actually breathe under water. I finally started to get the hang of it but still wasn't all that comfortable.

During the actual filming, I had to stand up to my waist in very cold water and wait for "Action!" As the cameras filmed the sinking ship I had to dive under it and swim away. It was a cold and miserable day.

In 1983, I played Eric in the television drama series *Two Marriages*. The show ran only one season, but it gave me a taste of daily life on a television show—and even better, a life without auditions.

One of my jobs interrupted a family camping trip to Illinois. Just as we pulled up the camper, I received the call to appear on the television show *Bret Maverick*. So Mom and I flew back to Los Angeles while Dad and the girls enjoyed a great road trip together. They went to Mt. Rushmore without me.

One thing I thought was really cool is that we got a *fax machine* in our house to have scripts sent to us ahead of time! Okay, it's not a big deal now, but in the days before cell phones and email, only the fanciest offices had these special machines. They rolled out difficult-to-read, blotchy information on rolls of thermal paper. When that baby started to hum, we all paid attention, wondering what exciting script might roll out.

As I reached puberty, I emerged from the "I can't stand girls, get them away from me" into the world of being smitten by them. I played the little brother to Michele Greene on an after-school special called *Andrea's Story: A Hitchhiking Tragedy*. I guess she was about 21. I watched her the entire time we filmed and developed a mad crush on her. The last day, I was so sad I was leaving and would never see her again. She stood off to one side talking to a friend. I shyly stepped over and stuttered, "Good-goodbye."

She gave me a courtesy smile. "Oh, goodbye, sweetie. It was really nice meeting you." Then she turned away and continued talking to her older friend.

I was crushed. Crestfallen. Heartbroken, I walked away.

I first met Tracey Gold when we played brother and sister in a McDonald's commercial. We met again in the made-for-television movie *Beyond Witch Mountain*. Later she played a cheerleader while I played a football star in the Robin Williams/Kurt Russell film *The Best of Times*. She was cute, she was good and she was always working on something. I had a bit of a crush on her at the time—which probably sounds a bit creepy to the rest of the world who think of us as siblings.

Chapter 5

Not the Sharpest Knife

1985

Mom screeched to a stop in front of ABC studios. "It's on the second floor. Run! See if you can still get in."

I bolted from the car. If I missed this audition, it would reflect badly on Mom—and even worse, on the prestigious, intimidating Iris Burton. We couldn't afford to lose the best agent in town.

I took the stairs two at a time. At the top, I pounded on the door.

A balding man opened it and peeked at me.

"Hi, I'm Kirk Cameron. I know I'm late . . ."

"You are," he said. He looked at his watch. "The audition was at 4:30. It's 5." He started to close the door.

Instinctively, I put my foot out so he couldn't close it. "I know, I know. But my mom will kill me if I don't do this audition. Please can I read just to tell her I did it?"

He looked over his shoulder, probably to ask what the others thought, then opened the door.

I had no idea what I was auditioning for except that it was a "pilot"—the first episode of a TV series that determines whether the network will put the show on its schedule. I'd gotten the script ahead of time but had really only glanced at it. I knew nothing about the show. To me, the title *Growing Pains* sounded dramatic and gritty.

I left the audition without a sense of how things had gone. They laughed, but I wasn't sure they were supposed to. Mom waited in the receiving room. "How did it go? How did you do? Was it okay that you were late?"

I did my usual shrug, but thought she should get a little more than usual because of the stress I'd put her through. "They laughed."

"That's great, Kirk!"

By this time, auditions had been coming fast and furious. Some panned out, some didn't. Mom really wanted me to get either a part in a series or the lead in a movie. She believed that at 14, I was ready and needed to take the next step in my acting career. One of my recent auditions was for the starring role in the movie *Lucas*. It had gone well and their first choice, Corey Haim, was not able to take the part. We had been told to wait by the phone for the announcement of my big break, but the call never came. I didn't get the *Lucas* job and I could tell Mom was disappointed.

"Maybe you'll get the pilot," she sighed.

I did get the callback for *Growing Pains*. This time I knew it was a comedy and played it the way I saw Mike Seaver.

It must have gone well.

One day I was playing Atari when Mom interrupted my session. "Kirk," she said, sticking her head in the room. "You got it! You got the pilot!"

> Kirk started getting laughs almost immediately . . . he was blow-you-away fabulous, he had enormous humor, enormous charm. When he finished, he looked at me and asked, "Is this supposed to be a comedy or what?" The entire room broke into laughter. The moment he left the room, we all looked at each other and said, "Teen idol." People get skeptical when they hear that. But I say to them that if you don't have an instinct in a moment like that, you are in the wrong business. As we talked further about him, we quipped about his question: "Yeah, he may not be the sharpest knife in the drawer, but he sounds like our Mike—clueless and adorable, charming and endearing."
>
> Mike Sullivan, Executive Producer of *Growing Pains*

I was happy and all, but her interruption caught me off-guard and Pinky cornered my Pac-Man before I could eat a power pellet.

Making the Show

Because I had been on the show *Two Marriages*, I had experienced life on a series. It wasn't all that new to me, though I played a bigger role in *Growing Pains* and, of course, one was a comedy and the other a drama. I was looking forward to it. You couldn't beat the steady work—and *no more auditions!* Of course, I would see a lot less of my friends, but I figured a comedy would be a lot of fun. At 14, I was ready for this new adventure, however long it lasted.

I knew that booking a pilot is only the first step to stardom—the network has a strong say in the final casting. It's a challenge to create a convincing "family" by throwing a group of strangers together. Actors have to possess that over-used adjective, *chemistry*. The children should at least resemble the actors playing their parents. (Whether I look more like Joanna Kerns or Alan Thicke, that's a puzzler TV historians can debate for centuries to come.)

Reading in front of the network bigwigs is much more intimidating than reading for the casting director. The room was bigger and we performed the audition on a stage. Thanks to the invention of shoulder pads, there were a lot of broad-shouldered suits scrutinizing us. Comedy is serious business.

The network picked up the pilot and we taped it, but in test screenings, the show didn't rate very well. Viewers weren't fond of the original Carol, and didn't like some of the banter between the parents. They felt it was mean-spirited, and *Roseanne* hadn't yet "set the Barr" for mean.

In response, Mike Sullivan put together an introductory piece to make the family more likeable. He also reworked the banter and cut together a little dual narration to show before the credits. They hired Tracey Gold to replace the original actress and we re-shot the scenes with her as Carol.

When the studio re-tested the show, *Growing Pains* was the top pilot for that season.

All-Star Cast

Alan

When I heard Alan Thicke would play Jason Seaver, I was excited. I knew he'd been a Canadian talk show host so I presumed he would be the star of our show. He was *the* name that would sell the show. (Though he had just experienced a disaster as host of *Thicke of the Night*, a late-night chat-fest that was supposed to take on Johnny Carson.)

I liked Alan immediately. He was funny, smart and witty—three traits that make it easy to comically play off someone else. Playing opposite someone as gifted as Alan made it easier for me to become Mike Seaver.

Alan was always extremely generous with his compliments about fellow cast members. Once in an interview he said, "Successful family shows need someone with that magic—the look that has the chance to take the country by storm. Michael J. Fox did that. Kirk seemed to have that. I thought, *This is a good rocket to hitch my star to.*"[1]

Joanna

Joanna Kerns became my second mom. *TV Guide* once had a cover shot of me, my mom and Joanna (who resembles my mom a lot) with the caption, "My Two Moms." They were holding flowers and I was the proud son.

I looked up to Joanna from the start. She was an experienced actress who had been in many movies. And she was pretty—though as a teen, you're really not supposed to think that of your "mother." When we met, she turned to my real mom and said, "Is it okay if I hug him? Can you hug a 14-year-old?" And so she did.

Like any proud mama would, Joanna also showered me with encouraging compliments. In the early years Joanna gushed, "Besides being just adorable, Kirk was a naturally gifted comedian. He didn't need to know what his 'motivation' was. He just did it. I thought he was really special."[2]

Tracey

I was really glad when my former crush, Tracey, joined the show. She looked a lot like my sisters and it wasn't long before I started treating her like one.

She was always smiling, innocent—kind of sheltered and naïve to a lot of worldly things. Because she'd been working since she was a toddler, she was actually the most experienced actor in the cast.

The girl could cry on cue, which was very impressive and hard to do. Witness the dramatic fourth season episode when Mike tells Carol her boyfriend just died. It was a magnum opus on-screen breakdown. I'm sure those scenes are what got Tracey all that dramatic work in TV movies after *Growing Pains*.

One of the funniest and most endearing things about Tracey was that she was so gullible. If you told her the word "gullible" wasn't in the dictionary, she would believe you. (We tried it once and it worked.)

Jeremy

For so long on the show, Jeremy Miller (who played Mike and Carol's little brother, Ben) was just a little tiny squirt. With his chubby cheeks and squinty eyes, he was our on-set chipmunk.

He loved a good practical joke as much as I did, and we loved conspiring together. When I needed an accomplice, he was right by my side. We were pals. He was the fun little brother I never had. He loved being on the show so much, he cried before each hiatus, not wanting to leave his second family.

"Mike"

I thought my character was the most fun to play, but he was also exhausting. I developed a way of coping with the high energy it took to play Mike Seaver. All the times I had shut down in the car on the way to and from auditions taught me how I could go into a quiet space in the midst of chaos. During short moments between takes or rehearsals, I sat in my chair, closed my eyes and zoned out. For a while people thought I was depressed and asked my parents about it, until they learned it was my way of recharging my Energizers.

A Week on the Set of *Growing Pains*

On Day 1 of a typical week, 50-some people gathered in an old house near the set. Coffee breath hovered in noxious vapors. Muffins, donuts and croissants were clutched in napkins. Idle chatter rattled and echoed in the room before the executive producers arrived.

Some hardworking P.A. (production assistant) had positioned 10 tables into a giant rectangle. Alongside other cast members, I pulled up a chair to begin our first read-through.

Another exhausted P.A. had driven through the night, all around town, to toss new scripts on the doorsteps of our houses. This was to give us time to read the script and prep ourselves for the table read. (I, however, was notorious for not reading the script beforehand. The writers began writing quips along the way: "Since Cameron hasn't read this yet . . .")

As the cast read through the script, the writers always looked a bit angst-ridden, eager for laughs. Who can blame them? This material was the baby they'd worked hard to push out. They really wanted the rest of us to love the baby, too. It wouldn't be enough to call their baby "cute"; they wanted to hear the words "hilarious" and "side-splitting."

After the read-through, everyone gave notes to the writers—suggestions on scenes, things we felt could be better. I'm sure the writers valued each and every note us actors gave them (or not).

On Day 2, a skeleton crew drifted onto the set sometime around 10 A.M. New scripts—printed on a different colored paper so we could tell which version we were on—were stacked on the Seaver living room coffee table. After a quick flip through the changes, we did a quick read-through before walking it out on the set. The director's job was to decide where the characters needed to stand and move—to figure out what looked most natural.

Tracey, Jeremy and I had to put in our three hours of school throughout the day, so stand-ins played our parts while we hit the books. The stand-ins took notes on each change the director made, then relayed those to us later.

At the end of the day, the writers and executive team returned to watch us put on the revised play, after which there was another note session. The writers, much less battered than the day before, once again trudged off to their room to incorporate the latest changes.

On Day 3 there were again new scripts delivered in a new shade of pastel. Lunch was often ordered in from our favorite restaurants and sometimes we all went out to lunch—either splitting up or going as a group if we could agree on the same place. (I was game for anything, as long as it wasn't raw oysters or loose flan.)

Day 4 found us "blocking" and taping the show. With our final script in hand, today was about rehearsing for the technical crew—lighting, camera and sound. Oftentimes, we performed the scene only once for the techs, then hit the schoolbooks. Stand-ins worked overtime on these days, performing the scenes over and over because that kind of rehearsal tends to exhaust the material for actors. No one wanted us to lose our "freshness of delivery."

This was by far the most tedious day, so the jokes started flying and pranks happened. Poking fun at others helped the day go faster.

On shoot day, Day 5, we rolled in around noon. Excitement was in the atmosphere. This was it, the big proving ground. Either we had it or didn't.

We rehearsed the entire show as many times as possible between noon and 4:00 P.M., shooting two takes on camera without an audience. Those versions were saved in case things went terribly wrong with the audience. A laugh track could always be used if a joke fell flat.

After a delicious four-course catered dinner, we lined up for makeup re-touching, hair re-dos and wardrobe refinements. No one wanted a lint-covered, frizzy-haired actor on camera.

Outside, several hundred people lined up, waiting to watch their favorite show being filmed. Executive producer Mike Sullivan remembers, "The tape nights were a mini-version of Beatle-mania; girls jumping up and down screaming . . ."

It was embarrassing. Well, just a tad. It *could* be really fun to walk out by the line and greet people. This really stirred up the fans and made 'em nuts.

When the doors opened, the audience was ushered into bleacher seats. A warm-up comic told jokes and did silly things to loosen everyone up. "How many folks drove over 50 miles to come see us?" he'd ask before hurling Tootsie Rolls at the crowd. Sugar never hurts comedy.

The audience got to see the show twice—including all the mistakes and re-takes. The best mistakes were saved for the gag reel at the end of the season. I, naturally, never made one mistake in all seven years. [Clears throat.]

Around 10 P.M., we wrapped the show and headed home.

The next day a car or jet would escort us away to a car show, mall, parade or other publicity event somewhere around the country. People imagine that being on a show is so glamorous, when mostly it's a lot of repetitive, tedious work. Fortunately, we had a great cast and crew who really got along and cared about each other. For me, it was never boring. There was a routine, but something different to do every day—a new scene, a new take on a joke, a new way to make something funnier. I had so much fun. The people I enjoyed most— my friends—were there.

My Competition

To the outside world, it may have seemed that I was in some kind of "teen idol showdown" with the likes of Michael J. Fox. Which one of us commanded the most fan letters? Who had more lunch pails with his face on them? How many times had each of us graced the cover of *BOP* magazine?

Those had nothing to do with the real competition between Michael and me.

Michael and I had this one-upmanship thing: who could incorporate the most 360s in a show. We'd have to walk onto a set and somehow do a complete, 360-degree turnaround. But we had to spin so naturally it was undetectable to our directors. We had to find a reason for our characters to do a 360. And it only counted if it made the final cut of the show.

Since our shows taped on different days of the week, some of the *Growing Pains* crew worked simultaneously on *Family Ties*. A cameraman would come to the set on blocking day and say, "Cameron, Fox did *two* yesterday."

"That's nothing," I'd scoff. "I can top it." I had to think of places to sneak them in. It was a fun challenge.

Sometimes the cameraman would go to the other set and say, "Fox, you're slacking. Cameron did four this week."

I think four was the record—but I'm not sure who set it. (Now that you know the real competition, look for our masterful 360s in re-runs.)

Another great Michael memory was the day he showed up in his hot convertible and somehow got me out of class. We tooled around town, pulling up next to cars filled with girls. Flashing our dual heartthrob smiles, those babes got a two-for-one special.

The average American seems to think that all stars know each other and hang out together. A day like that really played to *that* misconception.

As Long as We Got Each Other

From almost the beginning, the Seavers seemed like a real family. We teased, laughed and played pranks on each other. When the producers called "Cut" and the boom mic was still running, they'd listen to our banter in the control room. It sounded exactly like the conversation you'd hear in a real family.

"Jeremy, stop eating that. It's a *prop*."

"I can do what I want, Tracey."

"Jeremy likes to taste anything that's not nailed down," I quipped.

"Leave him alone, you two," Joanna instructed, just like any good mother. She was a hugger—my favorites were the times she embraced me with a motherly sympathy, like when I delivered a line badly and the entire crew was falling down with laughter.

Alan could regularly be found sitting on the living room sofa, eating the crunchy tops off the muffins from the Craft Services table. He was kind enough to leave the nasty, half-eaten bottoms for the rest of us. He loved to scan the reviews for the show or relay bits of show business gossip. "Hey, Joanna," he'd say. "I was watching *Entertainment Tonight* last night and they were profiling fabulous actresses who are also mothers. How come you weren't on there?" A comment like that would ignite a playful exchange—their real-life flirtation really strengthened the dynamic of their on-screen marriage.

The family relationships were not confined to the cast of five, but reached out to include everyone on the crew. Our director, John Tracy, told so many funny stories from his life in Brooklyn. He often started his stories with, "Our neighborhood was so tough . . ." and concluded with something I'd never experienced in my safe, suburban upbringing.

Alan and Joanna were both newly divorced single parents, and the set was always filled with their kids, my sisters and Tracey's and Jeremy's siblings. It was an army of noise whenever anyone had a birthday party, or during a seasonal party like Halloween or Christmas.

Every tape day, the cast and crew waited eagerly for my mom's special chocolate-chip cookies. They melted in your mouth—they were "like buttah" (which makes sense, as that was a main ingredient). Mom made dozens and dozens of them to make sure there were always enough to go around. I think she made 38 dozen a week as a thank-you for all the hard work the crew did.

Someone somewhere along the way started the Gum Wall. Folklore says it was me, but I don't remember—though I admit, it sounds like something I would have done. Personally, I think Jeremy did it. I suppose that whoever it was got caught at the last moment, realized that he needed to be onstage *now*, forgot to remove the gum from his mouth, and impulsively stuck it on the backside of the Seaver living room wall. It didn't take very long before everyone else decided this was a great place to stash his or her gum, too. For years, the blob grew until it looked like a giant, multicolored tumor. Alan says we should have sold it on eBay. Too bad no one thought of saving the sick monstrosity.

Don't Waste Another Minute on Your Cryin'

As a performer, I enjoyed drawing out tears—of laughter.

My on-set nickname was "Devil Boy," and it was anyone's guess when I'd strike again. Pranks were Devil Boy's mission. I was known to steal keys and hide cars in bushes on other sets. There was the "Morning glory" stink bomb that wafted its lovely odors from underneath the bleachers on tape night (usually during a "Carol" scene), the Vaseline on toilet seats, the snakes slithering onto set, the missing director's chairs that were eventually found hanging from the rafters, and the time when Alan the Muffin Man found all his muffin tops missing because Devil Boy had gotten there first.

Some of my best pranks were played on the cameramen. If I was feeling particularly devilish on tape night, I'd stealthily switch the focus and zoom cables on the cameras during our dinner break. When the cameramen were under the gun—live in front of the audience—trying to frame a close-up, the shot would simply go out of focus. When they'd scramble to re-focus, the shot would zoom in.

I also found that taping toothpicks to a wheel on the camera pedestal did a fine job of destroying a smooth dolly move to the right. The beauty of this stunt was that it was next to impossible to find the toothpick—not only because the wheels had covers, but also because there were three wheels the toothpick could be taped to.

Jeremy was my partner in crime, especially in school. We wrote notes and pinned them to the back of our teacher's corduroy jacket. The notes said things like "I hate puppies," "I wish I didn't work on *Growing Pains*," "Bring back the original Carol," and so on.

One note wasn't enough. The challenge grew and soon we were taping notes to the notes until the teacher had a tail 20 notes long, flapping around behind him as he went about our tiny classroom.

I noticed that phone techs could make a phone ring and asked one to teach me how. When the teacher wasn't looking, I punched in the code. When it rang, I said, "I'll get it."

"Oh, hi, John," I pretended to say to the director. Then I pulled out my disappointed voice. "But I just got back to school . . . uh-huh . . . well, as long as it's quick, I don't want to miss study time. I'll be right in." I hung up and turned to the teacher. "I guess they need me for a scene," and off I went.

Sometimes I took Jeremy and Tracey with me, borrowing a golf cart and charging off to the *Fantasy Island* set, which had dirt roads going into a jungle of banana trees, bamboo, pine trees and palms. We tried to catch some of the feral cats that prowled around in their own private world, mostly just attempting to get lost so no one could find us. Eventually we sauntered back to our jobs, innocent as lambs.

I could never really get in trouble, because, well . . . what were they going to do, fire me? That was the fun of it. Who was gonna get mad at the kid with the cute, crooked smile?

We're Nowhere Near the End

Although our long weeks made for a very exhausting life, every three weeks we had a week off and that helped. Sometimes I got burnt out, usually at the end of a season. I got tired of trying to learn new lines while hoping to forget the ones I'd just memorized a few days before.

Before we wrapped for the year, a film editor took clips from the show and other assorted set silliness to create a gag reel. Reflecting on the fun we'd had reminded us just how fortunate we were to be working with each other. (And hey, we weren't diggin' ditches or selling grapefruit by the side of the road.)

During the three-month hiatus breaks, I hung out at home, went on vacation with my family, and even went back to public school for a bit so I could keep up with my friendships. I also found time to shoot the films *The Best of Times, Like Father, Like Son, Listen to Me* and *A Little Piece of Heaven*.

The Best Is Ready to Begin

Those were good years. For a while, each season was more fun than the last. There was so much camaraderie between everyone—writers, directors, cast and the regular crew.

Alan Thicke appreciated the "genuine sense of family, which is especially important if you're raising kids and coming off a colossal, resounding failure. I loved the warmth, the positive-ness that comes from a successful show. I like what it stood for. Jason Seaver's values were close to my own. I often found myself saying things at home that I said on the show. Of course, it's easier to parent when you have eleven writers following you around."

Joanna Kerns said, "I loved coming to work every day. I loved playing a character I could live with. The security of that job for an actor opened so many doors for me. It changed my life. All we did is laugh. We had it so great."[3]

Notes
1. From an interview with Lissa Halls Johnson.
2. Ibid.
3. Ibid.

Chapter 6

TV's Best Kept Secrets

I lived in front of cameras during the stage when my Tic Tac-sized baby teeth were being replaced with chompers the size of Chicklets.

Being the model child that I was, I loved going to the dentist. Well, at least to "the Flipper King." Child actors were required to wear "flippers"—false teeth—that covered the mangy condition all developing mouths go through. A flipper was a kid-sized denture that fit in the mouth to fill in the missing teeth or to make teeth appear straight if they were naturally crooked. It was molded to fit perfectly to each specific mouth and give the wearer a smile that would make Joel Osteen jealous.

If it wasn't snug, the result was a lisp—and only Cindy Brady could pull that off. They were expensive, uncomfortable to wear and required many hours of rehearsal in front of a mirror to learn how to speak without showering people in spittle. Every time the size of my mouth changed (something I had very little control over), my mom had to cart me back to the Flipper King for a new, pricey set of flippers.

It was only the beginning of my education on selling product. Whether it was a food commercial, a detergent ad, a soft drink promotion or a cheesy infomercial, there was so much to learn about the art of the sale.

Hawkin' It

When I was little, I believed everything I saw on television commercials. Leprechauns made cereal with tie-dyed marshmallows, a bald man was responsible for cleaning products and a Jolly Green Giant harvested my corn. (Okay, I was gullible, but I wasn't Tracey Gold-gullible! I knew the difference between make-believe and real—though Bigfoot had me goin' for a little while.)

When I started working in commercials, I quickly learned some rules for hawking products:

1. Audiences like their soda in *frosty* mugs. It should look straight out of Santa's Village.
2. People respond to cereal floating in *foamy* milk.
3. When lapping up soup, viewers like to see kids dressed in cable knit sweaters by a fire.
4. A golden retriever in the background never hurt the sale of anything.

Another phenomenon I observed was the way advertisers embellished products to make them look more alluring. For example, in a cereal commercial, each Cheerio seen on camera was hand selected by a professional in the art of Food Props to ensure there was not a deformed O in the bunch. Sometimes he even sprayed them with shellac to really gloss 'em up. We were often warned not to eat the props.

All food designed to look perfect to the viewing audience was called "hero food." To create a heaping bowl of chili, marbles were hidden under the gruel to give it that extra chunky vibe. Hamburgers required "hero" pieces of lettuce and tomatoes. The art of melting a slice of cheese over the corner of a perfect burger is something film students can probably major in. The 50 replacement hero burgers were kept under lock and key like precious rubies. Dozens had to be prepped, as food wilted quickly under the bright, hot lights and dry air.

"Mmm, this burger tastes better than the ones they make in heaven!" I said, doing my best to really sell the awful scripted line.

"Cut!" the director barked, and that was my cue to regurgitate the hunk of meat into a spit pail. Instantly a team of professionals jumped into action.

Each person on the crew carried out an important part of the entire production. There were very specific departments, each belonging to their own union. If the food props guy was asked to move a book from one side of the set to the other, he refused—it wasn't his job. He had to get the set dresser to move it. If the actor touched the book, it became the responsibility of the props person. (Yes, props are different from *food* props.) There's a little saying that helped me keep things straight: *If it's on the set, it's set dressing. If an actor wears it, it's wardrobe. If someone touches it, it's a prop. If it's smoking, it's special effects. If it forgets its lines, it's an actor.*

Directors had trade secrets for selling product. During my white-water rafting Wrigley's gum commercial, the director taught us how to insert the gum into our mouths so it would fold in a visually pleasing way. We learned how to take a long piece of gum and get it to hit the tongue just right so it collapsed perfectly between our (fake flipper) teeth.

It didn't matter what it was we were selling, we had to look perfect and the product had to look perfect. Fortunately, we had lots of tricks up our sleeves to make that possible.

It didn't take long to learn that in Hollywood, make-up wasn't just for girls anymore. The bright stage lights made it necessary for even us manly men to put a little color on our faces. I sat in a tall director's chair, sometimes with my name ironed on the back—I felt Hollywood-cool. (If Evian water had existed in the '80s, I'm sure I would have demanded it with my bony index finger pointing to the sky.) It was great getting all that attention—people hovering over me to brush my hair or powder my face. I didn't have to do anything but sit there and enjoy the pampering.

The next room I entered smelled of Aqua Net. Hairspray was all the rage in the '80s. Even boys were under the influence of blown-out Farrah hair.

At some point, my face ceased to be as clear as a cloudless sky. Zits started popping up left and right, threatening to end my career as a doe-eyed pitchman. It wasn't so bad during the pre-teen years. But when I reached the age where it looked like sun-dried tomatoes were sprouting on my face, it was far more humiliating. "Wait a minute!" the make-up artist said before dipping into an industrial-sized tub of concealer to cover all my zits.

It only got worse when I became famous. In public, people would come up and say, "Wow, you don't have that many zits on *Growing Pains*." As a result, I spent a lot of time in my room, hiding from those comments and the embarrassment of my face.

Photo Op

Magazine photographers often came to my house on the weekends when I had more time to pose for their hunky photo spreads. My sister Bridgette said she hated waking up on a Saturday morning, bleary and wanting to stumble to the kitchen, to electrical cords snaking through the house. "Not again," she'd groan.

Some of the clothes they brought for me were cool—Ocean Pacific, IZOD, Members Only—but some of it was dorkier than the uniform my mom used to make me wear for auditions. The wardrobe stylists for these teeny-bopper mags dressed me in a jacket or sweatshirt with one sleeve rolled up over the shoulder to show my muscles. The photographer instructed, "Kirk, put your chin down. Now flex and peer out with a look that says 'I've got a secret.' That's it. Hold still, I think I see a hint of tricep!"

It cracked me up. Some of the posters made me look all steamy and sultry. I was a 14-year-old kid! What were the posters implying? I wasn't Don Johnson or Bruce Willis. I didn't have hair on my chest, like Hawaii-based PIs or men with talking cars. I'd never even been on a date.

My publicist wanted to break my Mike Seaver image and reinvent a new, edgy Kirk Cameron. When the stylist finished with me, I looked like a young Charles Manson on skid row, with an inclination towards transgenderism.

There are so many misconceptions about life as a celebrity.

False: *People think stars are unusual people.*

The truth is, actors are just like everyone else with the same vulnerable feelings, the same desire to be deeply known for who they really are.

False: *The work is really easy.*

There are long, hard days—sometimes 14 to 16 hours long. They can be physically and emotionally exhausting. On the other hand, the work *is* easier in some respects than many jobs. One director referred to his actors as "meat puppets." He implied that actors simply stand in front of a camera and deliver the lines someone else has written, performing them under the specific instruction of the director.

False: *It's a much easier life as a star.*

Financially that can be true. However, the old Beatle's song says it accurately: "Money can't buy me love." Money can create a zone of comfort but it can't buy happiness, love, true friends or character. The things that matter most in life cannot be bought at any price.

False: *Stars have no self-doubt or insecurities.*

If my reflections on my zit issues weren't convincing, I'll add this: Celebrities are the most insecure people I've ever met—and for good reason. Actors don't know if they'll have a job from one week to the next. They don't know if their eager, loyal fans will suddenly turn on them. Careers go up and down, and hopefully back up again (see Ben Affleck). Famous people don't know if the people who hang around them are true friends or just leeches trying to grab a free ride.

Hollywood takes insecurities and shortcomings and conceals them like pimples. False, phony images of "cool" are sprayed in the public's face like a bad gust of Aqua Net. The town shellacs the idea of "the good life" like it does each Cheerio, with the hope that you will buy what it's selling.

Chapter 7

The Perfect Family

One day not long after my sixteenth birthday party bash, Mom and Dad—both crying—sat us down in our home office. "Let's hold hands," Mom said, wiping tears from her face.

We reached for each other's hands, forming a group circle. The unusual gesture, along with the tears, caused my mind to race. What could possibly be wrong?

Mom took a deep breath. "We have something we want to tell you . . ." But her crying stole the words.

Dad looked at her, then at us. "Mom's going to be living someplace else now."

We sat, stunned.

My family looked idyllic to outsiders. It looked that way to insiders, too. Friends often commented how tight-knit we were. There was nothing that suggested to us that it would ever change. We had rules, curfews and expectations placed on us that clearly demonstrated our parents' love for us—and for each other. We got disciplined regularly. I look back now and think, *If they didn't really give a rip about me, they probably wouldn't have bothered.* It took time and effort for them to sit me down and talk with me before exercising discipline. It was an expression of their love and care for us. (Of course, when I was little, I didn't believe it for a moment when Dad said, "This hurts me more than it hurts you, son." *Then why isn't your butt pulsating, Dad?*)

While other child stars were suing their parents for millions, holding up liquor stores and ODing outside of nightclubs, we felt we were the lucky ones. Candace and I led the most glamour-less lives possible for kids on TV series. Our parents pushed for normalcy in every possible way. Bridgette and Melissa were the real stars of the family: Bridgette's dancing and singing talent combined with her charming personality and Melissa's first-rate brain and individuality made them two of the most well-adjusted teenage girls you could find.

Life suddenly became dreamlike and surreal. *My parents?* It couldn't be true. I'd heard about people getting separated and divorced, but never fathomed it could happen to our family. The announcement of my parents' separation didn't really sink in until I realized Mom had taken her clothes out of the house and was living somewhere else with a different set of furniture. Dad remained behind, miserable and heartbroken.

I lived behind the main house in a cottage Dad had built, so the day-to-day changes weren't supposed to affect me. But how could they not? My world had been turned upside down and shattered. I couldn't talk with either of my parents. Mom wasn't around anymore and Dad walked around in a daze.

I didn't feel I could talk to people at work, either. They were a nice surrogate family—I know, every actor says that about their cast. It's a cliché because it's usually true. The long hours on a sitcom create a familial camaraderie. Still, I didn't want Joanna, Alan, Jeremy or Tracey knowing about these real-life problems. I wanted to keep the façade that everything was okay. I didn't want to bare my family's failures in front of the world.

And, to be honest, I didn't know what the failures were. In my teenage mind, the Camerons were as ideal a family as the fictional Bradys or Cunninghams.

Real-Life Pains

At first I wondered if my role on *Growing Pains* or Candace's role on *Full House* were to blame. Had our work ruined the normal dynamic of an otherwise functioning family? Had the force of fame reframed everyone's lives? These were the very adult questions I asked, lying on my back inside my cottage apartment, becoming more withdrawn every day.

Dad had told Mom in the beginning that this Hollywood make-believe stuff was just that: make-believe. "Hey, Barb, this is great, this is fine, but let's not think this is going to last forever . . . because it's not," he warned. "And then the kids will have to go to college. We are *not* derailing college for a television show."

Both Mom and Dad told Candace and me that if we *ever* got puffed up about our celebrity, they would yank us from the business before we could say, "Don't you know who I am?!" Who we were as people was far more important than the perks that came with being on two hit television series.

Before the separation, our parents had attempted to keep life "regular" by having the whole family sit down to eat dinner as many evenings a week as possible.

We all had chores. I even had to keep my dressing room picked up, even though Warner Bros. hired maids to do that for us.

Whenever work demanded travel, Mom exchanged our First Class airplane tickets for as many coach seats as she could get so that one or more of my sisters could come along. If there was a local event, everyone came.

Mom brought my sisters to the set after school where Joanna's daughter and Alan's kids also hung out.

Our family vacationed in a cabin at Big Bear Lake where we tried to go as often as possible.

We didn't buy a huge mansion. We didn't put in a pool. We didn't drive flashy cars—although my mom once splurged on a vanity plate that read "STRZMOM." We didn't buy fancy furniture or clothes. We ate turkey tacos almost every night.

Fundamental Differences

Though Mom and Dad had seemed to stand in unison on all moral issues, I started to realize they had some fundamental differences.

When it came to religion, Dad had told Mom he wanted his children to choose their own religious paths in life. That statement laid the foundation for my earliest religious choice: to be a full-fledged atheist. I was convinced that God didn't exist, and my dad was fine with that conclusion.

Mom, on the other hand, believed in God. Yet she never really brought the subject up, except once. When I was a young teen I came home from school ravenous. I looked in the refrigerator. It was empty. I think I said "G—damn it" and kicked the fruit drawer.

"*What* did you say?" Mom asked.

"What?"

"What did you say?"

I just looked at her. I knew she'd heard me.

"Don't you *ever* disrespect God's name again," she instructed.

I was stunned. I thought, *That's weird . . . come on.* I couldn't remember ever hearing her mention God. No one talked about God in our family—ever. But the ferocity of her conviction made an impression on me and I never took God's name in vain again—at least not within earshot of my mother.

As I retreated from society both in my cottage at home and in my dressing room at work, I reflected on other things that could have caused "cracks" in my parents' marriage.

Dad didn't struggle speaking his mind. He spoke bluntly and plainly, often demonstrating an inappropriately critical personality. Before the separation, Dad criticized Mom and the girls a lot. He talked about their weight, even keeping a chart where he marked their weekly weights and monitored their food intake. His harsh words tore into them continually. His tone with Mom often insinuated she was simple-minded and fat. No matter what Mom did, she didn't feel she could measure up to what he wanted.

And so she left to try her hand at a new life.

It was a brutal six months for all of us. It doesn't sound like a long time, but in the life of a splintered family, it's an eternity.

My dad, shattered by Mom's exit, began to work hard at becoming the husband who could be kind and caring toward his wife.

Through many months of counseling with Rick, our family friend, my dad began the process of self-examination and rethinking what it means to love someone. He began to put his time, energy and resources into his relationship with Mom—planning special trips alone together, listening to her as she shared her thoughts and feelings, and learning to support and encourage my mom instead of demeaning and criticizing her.

When *Growing Pains* filmed in Hawaii for a second time, Dad gave Mom a new wedding ring set, asking her to rejoin him. All of us were astonished by the change in Dad. He grew to be much more loving and tender with Mom. He bought her gifts and spoke to her in a sweet voice. He became a different husband—and we all reaped the benefits of his maturity.

Chapter 8

My Teen Journal

> Today my buddies came up to Big Bear Lake and we had a great snowball fight! We played pool at the Gold's and Pictionary at the house. The girls made dinner and the guys had to clean up.

So reads my teen journal. I wrote a lot of things down as a kid (something that would come in handy one day when writing my autobiography). The thing that strikes me most, re-reading these old diaries, is how mundane and ordinary my life was during the crazy period.

> We played cards . . .

> We slid down the mountains on our brown lunch trays! Fun! Fun! Fun! Oh, and the night before we bought matching sweatshirts.

> I got in a fight with my dad . . .

My down time was filled with talking for hours on the phone, caring for my snakes and tarantulas, working out at the gym and getting grounded for talking back to my parents.

Of course, my life wasn't completely run-of-the-mill.

December 13, 1987

Went to breakfast at Jack's Deli . . . We [a
friend and I] talked for a while before we had
to go to the parade in Chatsworth. I was the
Grand Marshal. I rode in a white '57 Rolls
Royce. It was fun. After the parade, I wrote
Christmas cards and went to dinner.

January 24, 1988

Went to do the "Phil Donahue Show."

January 30, 1988

Strange day! This morning went to traffic
school. Very good learning but the other kids
couldn't care less. That lasted to 3:00 p.m. I
came home and tried to find a white shirt to
wear for the award show tonight . . . I ended
up wearing a black suit and tie and cummerbund.
We had to pick up Tracey and Jeremy on the
way down to the American Cinema Awards.

In some ways I was more mature than kids my age, and in others,
I lagged behind. I had traveled all over the world, met and hobnobbed
with the famous, managed my own career, hired my mother as my employee, bought a house at a very young age, and negotiated deals with
my agents who, in turn, negotiated with studios on my behalf. From
early on, I dealt with most adults on a level where I had more power
than they did. I held down a job that required long hours. I got there
on time, responsibly, and did the best job I could.

On the other hand, my reality was skewed. My immaturity resulted
from a sense of importance laid on me by nearly everyone I encoun-
tered. I lived in a closed world where my words were scripted. I was told

where to stand, when to move, how to look, what to wear. I was told when to arrive on the set and when I could leave.

I spent the bulk of my days with a pretend family whose issues always worked out in less than half an hour. We always dealt with conflict in a funny, heartwarming, positive way.

These don't transfer to the real world of relationships.

As much as I tried to be a kind, generous listener, I'm sure my social skills were lacking. I imagine I was clumsy, abrupt, selfish and moody. I'm sure I made some quick decisions, oblivious to the consequences.

I wasn't always sure how to deal with difficult relational situations because I had been shielded from so many. People in my professional life never dared to oppose me. They gave me whatever I needed whenever I asked for it. If I spoke, they listened. I was always right. Whatever made my life on the set more comfortable, I could have.

I had enough money to do as I wished, but not enough life skills to relate to people in a healthy way or to perform ordinary tasks such as managing my time, balancing a checkbook or creating and following a schedule.

The Introverted Idol

I didn't like unfamiliar people or surroundings. I felt very off-kilter, shy and uncertain—the irony being that my career depended on my ability to talk to unfamiliar people in unfamiliar surroundings. One of the most private kids around was one of the most recognizable people in America.

It probably would have shocked my fans to find out how self-conscious I was at the height of my idol-dom. On August 1, 1987, I forced myself to create a self-confidence project, hoping to increase my self-esteem, by listing my positive traits as I saw them.

I am a healthy person. I am very sensitive to others' problems. I am an honest person, I am a good actor, I am an affectionate person, and I like to be open to suggestions and ready for a change if needed.

I was embarrassed by how I looked—you already know about my zits. My paranoia grew when I discovered "Cameron" literally means "crooked nose." I went straight to the mirror, examined my nose from every angle and realized with horror that my nose didn't go straight down between my eyes—it went diagonally.

All I could think about was my stupid crooked nose.

I fretted over how ugly I was and wondered why anyone would want to be around someone so gross. Trying to be helpful, Dad said, "You're on the cover of 14 magazines this month. Obviously somebody doesn't think you're ugly."

When a normal person runs into other normal people, both people ignore common defects in each other—it's common courtesy. If a woman has a curling iron burn on her forehead, you don't bluntly ask, "Is that a hickey on your brow?" If a guy has a bump on his lip, you don't point at it and say, "Is that a cold sore on your lip? Whose face have you been kissin'?"

But as a celebrity, my looks were open for discussion. Strangers loved to point out anything on my face that seemed awry: zits, blackheads, freckles, pimples and that stuff that forms in the corner of your eyes when you're asleep. All of it was pointed out to me—and did nothing for my self-confidence.

I used to tell my parents how awful I felt about myself and they would say, "Every teenager feels that way. It's no big deal." The most I got was a trip to a dermatologist to get tetracycline.

I became kind of a loner and somewhat depressed. I didn't go out with my friends. I desperately wanted to, but it was too hard to come home from work where people did *not* make fun of me, to kids who were ruthless as only teenagers can be. I also felt like I was living in a fishbowl, that everyone was whispering, "Boy, he's so different in person . . . and his skin is so much worse than it looks on TV."

I installed red light bulbs in my dressing room and dimmed them. The red light canceled out the red marks on my face. Talk about looking at the world through rose-tinted glasses . . .

At one point I brought make-up home from the set so I could camouflage my facial glitches and look more like Mike Seaver if I absolutely had to go out. One day Mom gently said, "Uh, Kirk, honey . . . guys don't wear makeup off-camera. I think you should draw the line at Clearasil."

Hanging in my bedroom alone was easier than going out and keeping up an image.

The Health Nut

January 23, 1988

I ate at The Good Earth. I had to get ready for the Golden Globe Awards. I went with Mom, Dad and Iris. I was nominated for the first time!!! For a supporting role in a series. I didn't win though . . .

I was a quirky one. I loved eating at my favorite restaurant, The Good Earth, every chance I got.

No one could believe it when I chose to go on the Pritikin diet as a young teenager. (At least it gave *BOP* magazine something new to write about.) The reason I started the diet was that my greatest fear in the world was getting arteriosclerosis. The moment I heard about this horrible disease, I could feel my arteries hardening to plastic. I figured I'd keel over and die at any moment. To delay my impending death (and also to help my mom lose weight by supporting her), I went on the Pritikin diet and became a vegetarian. I ate only the whites of eggs and the staple of my diet was tofu.

Combined with the healthy diet thing, I was a germaphobe. I would *never* eat something off of somebody else's plate. If my dad ever took a bite of my food off my plate, I'd push my plate away, disgusted—and done. I also never drank from someone else's glass. I kept picturing all that backwash.

I was naturally skinny. Because of that embarrassment, and because of my zeal to be healthy, I was obsessed with going to the gym. Every day I worked out for two hours after school or work.

No matter how much I tried to bulk up, I was always the skinniest guy at the gym. I thought, *I'm skinny and I have horrible skin. Who will ever want to go out with me?* Malcolm Jamal-Warner from *The Cosby Show* didn't seem to share my affliction.

When I turned 16, I began to confide in the man who had cut my hair since I was 9, the stylist Fran Rich had recommended. Rick Eichhorn became my closest friend for several years. I think one of the reasons I appreciated Rick was that he never once mentioned anything about my skin or my scrawny build. He was just a friend. I felt very comfortable hanging out with him and talking with him about anything. I didn't have to hide from him. Rick was my best friend at a time when I really needed someone to confide in.

Hair Today, Gone Tomorrow

When I was little, my hair was blonde and as straight as uncooked spaghetti noodles.

One day in my early teen years I was at the beach, using baby oil to get a deep, dark tan. (I may have feared arteriosclerosis, but I thought nothing of skin cancer.) When I got home from the beach, I looked in the mirror to discover curly hair atop my head, as if I had gotten a perm. I chalked it up to it being sticky from the baby oil, salt, sand and air.

After a quick shower, however, my hair remained curly. Forget Malcolm Jamal-Warner—my hair started to look like Lisa Bonet's!

Not for that reason, but I kind of liked it. Mom wasn't so sure. She hovered over me—making me feel like the mama's boy I was—blow-drying the heck out of my hair. She wanted it straight for interviews and auditions.

One day I finally said, "Mom, no more blow-drying. I want to leave it like this."

I went to Rick and said, "Do something with this mop-top." He cut and messed with it until I had a loose, curly mullet thing going on—short on the sides, long in the front, long in the back. (Hey, don't laugh. Mullets *made* Billy Ray Cyrus—and now he's got his own little teen star, Miley, to deal with.)

Guy Gone Mild

March 19, 1987

It's really weird that out of all the people in the world, I, Kirk Cameron, don't have a girl-friend. Everyone seems to think that I'm sooooo lucky and could have any girl I want. But the problem is, I haven't found anyone yet. I just want someone to love and to love me back. I feel like I'm really missing something in my life. Someday, though, I'll find her. I just can't help but ask myself, "Why me?"

My nephew loves to cover his body in bling. He impresses chicks with his sports car. His dream is to be in the shoes I was in at 16. He recently asked, "What was it like, Kirk? I mean, *dude*! You coulda done *anything*. Tell me you took advantage of this somehow. Give me the juicy details. This is, like, my dream."

I guess in the eyes of many, I blew it. I didn't go out with all the babes. Contrary to *National Enquirer*, I did not buy my home in Simi Valley to line the walls with women. Maybe I had a smorgasbord of women to choose from, but I was never a playboy. My friends couldn't believe how I didn't take advantage of all that female energy rushing in my direction.

I went to Tracey Gold's prom with her—as friends. I had escorts to movie openings or awards ceremonies—as friends. Sure, I had a crush on Alyssa Milano from *Who's the Boss?*. What teenage guy didn't? But crushes were the safe way out. You could have feelings for someone and still keep your distance.

My heart wasn't where Mike Seaver's was—or the bulk of the male population's. I never got a DUI because I didn't drink. The only thing I ever smoked was a ham for Thanksgiving. Maybe I would have had more free time to get into trouble with girls if I wasn't so busy killing rats to feed my snakes. All I wanted was to find *one* girl and be with her for life.

July 25, 1987

I really wish that I will meet someone that is
so special, and wants to be with me as much as I
want to be with her and who will be excited for
me about my career and will not be interested in
Kirk Cameron the actor, star of Growing Pains.
I'm looking for someone who could be my best
friend. Someone who is not the least bit phony
but who is just so honest and open about her
feelings and who genuinely cares about mine and
wants to share her feelings with me.

Not too long after I wrote that journal entry, I met a girl on the set.
She came in for a quick guest role, and we began seeing each other off
set. I grew very fond of her and her family—especially her father, who
later became very instrumental in answering my questions about God.

Within a year, my immaturity had made a royal mess of that relationship and left that sweet girl heartbroken and confused. She was
the last girl I went out with until the most breathtaking woman in the
world entered my life.

Chapter 9

I Fired My Mother

I never knew how much money I made during my early teenage years. I sensed I wasn't workin' for minimum wage, though. My job didn't involve cleaning the deep fryer or wearing a cone-shaped paper hat. I knew I could make in weeks what my father made in a year—which seemed insane considering how hard he worked.

My parents handled all my money. Some of my income paid for the high expenses of being in the business—incidentals such as headshots, taxes, agent fees, manager fees, lawyer fees, insurances and union dues. Much of it went into a trust account guided by a law that required parents to put a certain percentage away for their children. Dad increased that mandatory percentage and upped the age when I could get my hands on it, and he invested my money in a variety of places.

Sure, I would have enjoyed buying that private fantasy island. Yes, I would have enjoyed legally changing my first name to Gilligan and starting my own perfect civilization on that uncharted desert isle—but Mom and Dad knew better. They had foresight to realize I would handle my money better once I was older.

Mom became my manager when it was clear we couldn't afford the costs related to acting unless she got a full-time job. Someone needed to take me to the studio daily and stay there, because it was required by law that every underage kid have a parent or legal guardian around all day. It seemed silly to pay someone else to do that, so she took the job.

Mom was great on the set. Everyone loved her. She was never considered a "stage mom" and I liked that about her. Much like Mike Seaver had an attractive, likable mom in Maggie, I had the same in my real mom. Everyone loved Barbara Cameron.

She didn't shackle me or smother me with her love. Mom stayed in the background and made friends with the crew. She baked hundreds of dozens of her famous chocolate-chip cookies for all. She broke through the Hollywood games with her down-to-earth simplicity.

Barbara Cameron

In the beginning, I didn't look at it as a career for myself. I looked at it as a potential opportunity for my kids, whatever that panned out to be. I just wanted them to be happy. There was never anyone in our family who was involved in the business prior to our kids and so I was pretty green at what a parent's role was, other than to drive them to auditions and if they were lucky enough to book, then I would sit on the set and make sure that they were not abused or treated poorly.

Kirk

Eventually my parents started giving me an allowance more substantial than most kids had, based on my income. I usually took that cash to my bank (conveniently located next to Foster's Freeze) and stashed it away in my savings account. I kept my little red bank account book in a safe place, occasionally opening it to glance at the total. I couldn't believe how much money I had!

That $132 balance was my treasure, my loot, my booty. I was a squirrel whose nuts overfloweth'd.

Despite my desire to mastermind my own private island civilization, in truth, I was never a big spender. In most practical cases, I was a very frugal kid. When I finally purchased a sports car, I bought a Honda Prelude. It was a sweet ride, but not exactly the price of a Rolls or a Bentley or a Jag.

From ages 14 to 21, I was in a strange position of power, which made for a warped adolescence. A huge load of responsibility was dropped onto my shoulders when *Growing Pains* took off. Never having done it before, I didn't know how to be a kid and live like a responsible adult at the same time. I didn't know how to do all that was required of me and still be like a regular teenage kid. All I really wanted was to be normal. My way of dealing with the pressure of the business was to compartmentalize, so I didn't talk about business when I was home.

> Kirk and I never talked about work, ever. Our friends weren't on television shows. There was a point when I realized my brother was the only one who could relate to me on this aspect of our lives. I once asked him an industry question at home, wanting to kind of talk to him about it. I don't even remember what it was about—whether it was getting a different part, or an actual acting technique, or whatever. His answer was nice, but very short. He had absolutely no interest in talking about acting or the entertainment business at home.
> He was a very private person when it came to work.
>
> Candace Cameron, Kirk's sister

Playing someone popular—a "breakout character" they called it—gave me influence on set. I wasn't looking for that type of power; it just came with the territory. But even more confusing was the role I played with my own mother. At the age of only 14, I was my mother's employer.

She worked for me, in a twisted order of hierarchy. Professionally, I told *her* what I wanted and didn't want. I expected her to handle my appearances, schedule my auditions and manage my money.

I know that to most, having some kind of authority over one's parents sounds like a dream come true. "Here's how it's gonna go down, Ma." But it wasn't at all. I wasn't comfortable being my mom's boss or with the daily flip-flop of authority. I was supposed to be her employer on the set and her kid once I walked through the front door of our house. The power shifts were freaky and hurt my brain a little.

Barbara

Kirk was distant with me when I talked about business at home, so I came up with a plan to look different when I needed to play manager. I dressed in a suit and went to the set to see him. When he saw me in the suit, he knew there was business to attend to.

I tried to keep my commitment to just talk about work at work and not at home, but that didn't last very long. There were too many decisions that needed answers at a moment's notice.

Kirk

The whole situation became more uncomfortable to me when I turned 16 and could drive myself to work. I didn't think I needed a manager anymore, but it was my mother's career. The situation was getting messy, and I spent a lot of time trying to figure out what to do.

I had watched my mom change from being a relatively shy and insecure woman to a strong woman in her job as my manager. I didn't want to take that away from her. In a way, I felt my mom was dependent on *my* approval of *her*. I knew a good portion of her self-worth came from holding down this important job. She was finally building the confidence in herself she had always wanted.

I felt the weight of the world on my shoulders, like I was responsible for everyone's happiness—my mother's, my friends', the cast and crew, my fans and the entire nation of viewers who were relying on Mike Seaver to teach their kids right from wrong. The years of being "on" all the time began to suck away the joy and fun.

While being aware that I was responsible for everyone's well-being, I took a very difficult step—one I agonized over for some time. I can't remember how it happened, but I fired my mom.

Barbara

I remember when Kirk said he needed to talk with me. I had known this day would come and had tried to prepare myself for it. The way Kirk approached me was very sensitive. I remember him telling me that since he had a new agent, he didn't need me to manage his career anymore. His new agent would do that.

What meant a lot to him was the new camp he was starting, Camp Firefly. He asked me if I would still handle all the details of the camp for him. That eased the pain a bit.

It was hard to be "fired," but I think letting go of his affairs was a relief to some extent. It had been difficult to try and maintain a normal mother-son relationship with the work dynamic thrown in.

Kirk

Mom was gracious, but I bumbled through the conversation as only a teenager can—ineptly. There's no easy way to "let a parent go" from a job and I wouldn't wish that situation on anyone.

But what I really needed was a mom. I still wanted to take advantage of that free laundry service at home. I wasn't about to turn away the homemade potato-chip casseroles or her famous turkey tacos. I didn't even mind when the "chore chart" was put up on the fridge. That was the normalcy I craved. I wanted Mom to continue to bring warm cookies to the set, making me the guy with the best mom around.

Chapter 10

My Wild Side

Contrary to what you might think, Kirk Cameron had a side to him that was wild . . .

. . . *ish.*

Okay, I was pretty straight-laced, even from a young age. But that doesn't mean I didn't like a little adventure.

Like every boy, I really wanted a pet. But I was allergic to animal hair. I realize having "allergies" doesn't help my street cred, either. But this might: I ended up living amongst reptiles. That's cool, right?

I first got the idea while lizard hunting with Uncle Frankie when I was 10. We caught a black and yellow-striped garter snake and I kept that for a while. Later, I acquired a six-foot Burmese python and named him Dudley, after Dudley Moore, my co-star in the film *Like Father, Like Son*. The cast of *Growing Pains* gave me a red-tailed boa constrictor for my birthday one year and I named that one Glenn, after my cool set teacher. I had another red-tailed boa that I named Springsteen, named for—well, you can probably guess.

I put the snakes in my pockets, wore them around my neck and took them to school in my backpack. During recess or lunch I had a little following of snake lovers who would go with me behind the handball courts, where I brought them out.

My sisters loved the snakes. They draped them around their necks or put them around their waists like belts. Melissa and I laid on the futon bed, very still, and let them swarm all over us, just like River Phoenix in *Indiana Jones and the Last Crusade*.

As long as I kept them in the cage, Mom didn't mind my reptilian friends.

Until they got out.

Once somebody left the cage open and one of my slithery friends wrapped itself around the toilet bowl (giving new meaning to the phrase "snaking the toilet"). This was neither pleasant nor charming to my dear mother.

Sometimes they wrapped themselves around a doorknob or hid in the crevices of the couch. One slipped behind my dad's bathroom sink vanity into the wall. I grabbed it by the tail, but because snakes are all muscle and very strong, I couldn't get him out. After trying many different methods, we finally pointed a hair dryer inside the hole. In moments, it had heated up so much that he shot out of there, much like me at a stuffy industry event.

Murder

To feed my little reptilian herd, I bought rats from the pet store—until they got too expensive. A Japanese neighbor taught me how to catch rats in the hills by making a trap for them. The disgusting part is that I had to kill them before I fed them to the snakes, or the snakes could lose an eye (or worse)—rats are nasty little buggers when they fight for their lives. Case in point: One got out of the cage and bit me. I decided to fix him. In the garage we had a giant meat freezer. I put the whole cage in the meat freezer and a few hours later, he was a ratsicle, poised and ready to run.

(I kindly ask readers not to turn me in to PETA.)

For a while, I kept a stash of dead rats in the house freezer. Big deal. They're in plastic bags, right? Yet for some odd reason, Mom objected. I moved them to the outside freezer. When it was time for a meal, I thawed one or two out in the sun until they got nice and aromatic. Then I thrust them inside the cage and poked 'em with a stick to make them look alive. The snakes bought my little marionette show every time.

My sisters each had a pet hamster. The male got busy servicing the females and soon there were nine baby hamsters. There were so many babies, I figured my sisters wouldn't miss one. And my snake was hungry. *How good can Melissa be at math, really?*

Very good, apparently. Melissa was horrified when she walked in just as my snake opened his jaws and descended on her baby.

As the snakes got bigger, they needed too many rats, so I decided to feed them chickens. The downside was killing the birds—for some reason, murdering chickens was tougher on my psyche than rats.

Sex

Learning about sex was an adventure.

Mom and Dad didn't rush to bring it up. Mom remembers attempting a conversation with my sisters about sex as she backed out of the driveway. With all the sincerity she could muster, Mom said, "I want to talk to you about . . . the birds and the bees."

Bridgette said, "*Moooom*, we already *know* about all that stuff."

Surprised, Mom stopped in the middle of the street. "Really, where? Who told you about that?"

"Our friends, *duh*."

"That's supposed to be something moms talk about with their daughters," she said, disappointed.

"Shoulda brought it up two years ago, then," my sisters laughed.

I didn't get "the talk" either. Instead, I looked at the set of encyclopedias in our house and thought, *I wonder if the word "sex" is in there.* I took the "S" volume to my room and discovered that the word *was* there. So was an explanation. I longed to get back the image of a baby brought by a long-beaked bird—but life had changed. At 10 years old, innocence had been shattered. I remember reading the clinical details and thinking, *Oh, disgusting! There's gotta be a better way than that!* (I don't see it the same way anymore—for the record.)

Alcohol

At 16, I shot *Like Father, Like Son* in San Diego. As usual, Mom came with me.

One day, a bunch of us on the film went to Mexico for a day off. We ate at a restaurant where other under-aged kids were drinking margaritas.

I looked at Mom, my moral barometer. As much as I complained about her, I really respected her a lot. So when she shrugged and said, "It's up to you, Kirk," I figured this one time wouldn't be a big deal. And it wasn't. I don't think I drank more than a few sips.

That was the only alcohol I had as a minor.

Dirty Dancing

Uncle Frank took great pains to teach me how to dance. It was very kind of him, but his training didn't produce spectacular results.

At my first middle school dance, I couldn't even get up enough nerve to make it out on the floor. I went into the bathroom and practiced my moves in front of the mirror for at least an hour, with Debbie Harry pumping through the walls. When I came out, I still couldn't do it. It became my default position—hiding in the stalls.

I eventually warmed up to the whole slow dancing thing, but that was easy: All you had to do was hold on for dear life and sway.

Piercings

My big claim to walking the wild side happened when I was 15. The entire cast and crew had been flown to Hawaii to shoot *Growing Pains*. I wanted to do something crazy, like getting a tattoo or a piercing. Brian Peck (my stand-in), Brooks (my friend) and I decided to do something Insane with a capital *I*.

We strutted the streets of Honolulu, pondering our options. We settled on an ear piercing. A lightweight risk, to be sure, but I certainly wasn't going to stick a needle in any other body part.

Going into the store with a swagger, I thought, *Look out world, I'm gettin' pierced.*

Walking out I thought, *Oh, no. What's Mom gonna say?*

I shoved Brooks in front of me, making him go into our hotel room first, me tip-toeing behind. Mom took one look at him and

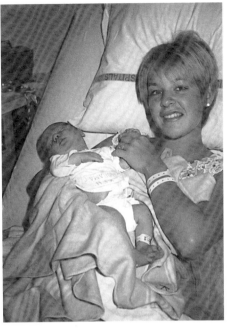

Mom with me at one day old (October 13, 1970).

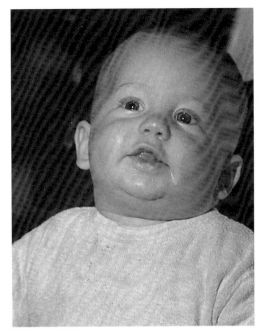

One of my first headshots.

Me at eight months old.

At the beach on one of many Sunday outings, here with Grandma Jeanne.

This is the photo of me wearing a mop on my head—the photo Aunt Joanne promised would never be shown. I was four years old.

HOLIDAY JOY

Left: Bridgette and me sitting in front of the apartment for our Christmas card that year.

My sister Bridgette and me holding our sister Melissa in front of our house.

Above left: Me at Busch Gardens on the boat ride at five years old.

Above Right: Mom, my sisters and me wearing the matching outfits she made for us.

Left: This family photo of me was actually used on one of the season openers on *Growing Pains*.

Below: Candace, Melissa, Bridgette and me posing for our Christmas card photo in 1978.

Another early headshot my mom had taken for me.

Me at age seven.

It was this picture of my sisters and me that persuaded legendary agent Iris Burton to give us an audition.

An early commercial I did with James Garner— it was a Polaroid camera commercial.

With James Garner on the set of *Brett Maverick.*

On the set of *Herbie, the Love Bug*, in 1982.

With Mariette Hartley on the set of another Polaroid commercial.

A shot taken for the Iris Burton Agency.

Above: When I picketed dad one day after I thought he was being too cranky.

Left: In my tuxedo for the Youth In Film Awards.

Below: My sisters and me before we attended the Youth In Film Awards later that night.

With Robin Williams, Kurt Russell and my mom on the set of *The Best of Times*.

With my mom and sisters at a Christmas event.

Michael J. Fox saying a few words at my sixteenth birthday party.

Trying my hand with the camera on a film set.

One of our family portraits: Mom, Dad, Melissa, me, Bridgette and Candace.

My high school graduation photo.

Singing with Bob Hope on one of several TV specials I did with him.

I joined Bob Hope on another TV special, *Bob Hope's High-Flying Birthday*, featuring President Ronald Regan (the special also featured Lucille Ball, Phyllis Diller, Brooke Shields, Don Johnson, Emmanuel Lewis, Elizabeth Taylor and Barbara Mandrell).

A recent photo with Dad.

Showing off my son James to Grandma Helen.

At my sister Candace and Valeri Bure's wedding.

Me and my sisters Bridgette, Candace and Melissa in spring 2006.

Ray Comfort and me on the set of our TV show *The Way of the Master*.

Chelsea with one of the campers at Camp Firefly.

In the early days at Camp Firefly.

A recent photo of Chelsea and me.

said, "Brooks! You got your ear pierced! It looks really good on you. Kinda cool."

She didn't freak. Maybe I'll be okay.

I walked around him and said, "Hi, Mom . . . what did you do this afternoon?"

Mom gaped in stunned silence.

Brooks and I busted up laughing, hoping that making light of it would go over better with Mom.

She stammered a bit. Because she always liked being a cool mom, I figured she was struggling between that and being really ticked at me.

"Well, at least you didn't get a tattoo," she said under her breath. "You can't get rid of a tattoo." She scowled, took a deep breath and put her hands on my shoulders so that she could look me directly in the eye. "Kirk, it's not that you got your ear pierced—it doesn't look bad. I even sort of like it. It's that you went off and deliberately did it without asking." She turned around and went into the other room.

I felt horrible.

She didn't talk to me for two days.

Fashion Crimes

Murdering chickens wasn't my only crime. I also broke laws in my choices of clothing.

Most of my clothes were chosen by someone else. I didn't have to worry about wardrobe on set—the costumer chose those. I blame him for any of Mike's embarrassments in couture.

I didn't have a costumer at home. At my junior high graduation, my friends wore dress shirts and slacks. I sported a white tuxedo shirt—the kind with tails hanging down to my knees—shiny snake skin pants and a bowtie fastened around my neck. Not around the shirt collar. Around my neck.

My favorite teen outfit (when left to my own devices) consisted of a Prince T-shirt, red high-tops and black parachute pants, legs pegged three inches over my ankles. I also had acid-washed jeans, of course. My sisters and I laid our brand-new jeans on the concrete driveway, got a bucket of bleach and splashed the jeans to make them look like spotted cowhide.

Murdered chickens, piercings, two sips of tequila, junior high restrooms, shameful choices in clothing—now you've seen the wild side of Kirk Cameron. Told 'ya.

Chapter 11

I Dissed Lucy

Somehow, I was the only one who missed *I Love Lucy* as a staple of my childhood. *Happy Days*—sure. *The Brady Bunch*—couldn't get enough. But *Lucy* must have run during my snake-feeding or sister-torturing sessions.

Looking back, my lack of TV history knowledge at that stage in my career is really embarrassing—especially because acting is my profession. I was making a lot of money from an industry with no appreciation of its pioneers.

Bob Hope invited me to be a part of a few of his TV specials. I only knew him as "the old dude who entertained the troops." At the taping of the first special, I found myself in my trailer, getting mic'd (the awkward part before any live performance, when a complete stranger runs his cold hand inside your clothes and burrows a wireless microphone in any crevice he can find). I was nervous about the show, trying to remember what Bob wanted me to do. My mom sat across from me in a recliner, eating a snack and reminding me of the lyrics to the song I would perform.

A guy poked his head through the door. "Mr. Cameron, Lucille Ball would like to meet you."

I didn't even know who this Lucille was. *Another crazed girl? Give me my peace!* I mumbled to myself. I couldn't believe someone would interrupt me during my prep time.

"I'm sorry, I'm busy right now," I shot back. "I'll get to her when I can."

My mother spit up a little of the caramel corn she was working on. "Kirk! You can't do that! You need to drop everything right now and go meet her!"

Moments later, another knock.

"Mr. Cameron, Miss Ball is here to see you."

Annoyed, I stepped outside to meet a wrinkly old lady. She wore a scary orange wig, the hue of a setting sun. "Hi, I'm Lucille Ball," she said in throaty voice that had taken a beating from tobacco.

"Nice to meet you. I'm Kirk," I said, shaking her hand.

I had no idea that this woman, along with her husband, Desi Arnaz, had pioneered the art of shooting a sitcom with three cameras (instead of one film camera). "Desilu" meant nothing to this teenage brain. If asked, I would have guessed it was a dance craze. The Foxtrot. The Macarena. The Desilu. But the star of the most successful comedy in TV history? Didn't ring a bell. I figured the broad was some old friend of Bob's—he must have felt sorry for her and booked her on the show to lift her spirits.

During the show, Lucy did a magic trick that involved pulling many strange objects out of the trunk. With her inimitably expressive eyes, she reacted to each item as she yanked it out. Finally, she pulled *me* out of the trunk.

Man, I was an idiot.

I missed the opportunity of a lifetime. Lucy was ready to have a casual conversation with me! I could have asked for tips. I could have kissed the feet of the sitcom queen—the same feet that stomped grapes to get a role in an Italian movie. I could have gotten advice from the lips that downed Vita-meata-vega-min, and inspiration from the woman whose nose was set on fire in front of William Holden . . . but instead, I was totally clueless.

I vaguely remember the rest of the conversation with Lucy. After she introduced herself, she said something like, "I've seen your work and you're very good."

"Thank you," I said smugly—just as I had a thousand times before to every other grandmother who thought I was adorable. I didn't offer any compliments in return because I didn't know who she was. Rather, I thanked her for her kind words and excused myself to go back into my trailer so I could take a nap.

My mom looked like she had seen a ghost. Her countenance froze like a freshly Botoxed face. Her son's profound ignorance had left her in shock.

That particular Bob Hope special included Brooke Shields, Phyllis Diller, Don Johnson and President Ronald Regan. If I didn't have a picture of me shaking hands with the President, I wouldn't have remembered he was there. I was more excited about meeting Brooke Shields than anyone else on the show. Ah, the priorities of a teenager.

Not too long after, Lucille Ball died. Bob Hope invited me to join him and others in a tribute show—all the greats of comedy were there. At the end of the night, I stood on stage, holding hands with some skinny old dude named Jimmy Stewart as the entire cast sang a song.

Afterward, Bob invited me to his home for dinner. I said to Mom, "Do I have to go?"

"*Yes!*" She and Dad looked at me as if I'd been lobotomized.

I climbed into a car with another old guy named Danny Thomas. He shouldn't have been behind the wheel. On the way to Bob's house, he opened his glove compartment to show me his gun. I wasn't sure why he did that, but it unnerved me a little. I had no problem "making room for Daddy" while this dude was sportin' a heater.

Inside Bob's house was an original Norman Rockwell painting of a much younger Bob, complete with his trademark ski-slope nose. His wife, Deloris, seated us around the table: Bob, Danny, Jimmy, Phyllis Diller, George Burns and me. I sat there, bored, thinking to myself, *If I wanted to spend time with seniors, I could've visited a convalescent home, entertaining them with my latex glove turkey trick.*

There was a lot of cackling, coughing and flapping dentures that night. I vaguely remember something about George Burns not being able to get a cat out from under his house. Phyllis Diller's laugh frightened me a little.

I think I did a total of three Bob Hope specials. When I look back on them now and remember myself in a sailor suit dancing like a monkey while Bob sang "One Hot Tamale," I wonder why such an honor was wasted on a knucklehead like me.

Lifestyles of the Rich and Famous

Some of the events and shows I participated in gave me life experiences I otherwise would never have had.

Though planes made me nervous, I always enjoyed the privilege of bringing along any friend I wanted—that was always part of the deal. It was a blast traveling with a buddy, seeing the world through bachelor eyes.

I usually flew commercial airlines, but there were a few flights in private Lear jets, which look exactly like they do in movies: luxurious living rooms in the sky. No matter how I got where I was going, if it was business related, the travel was all-expenses paid.

There were so many exciting trips, they started to blend together.

In Vancouver, Canada, there was a week-long celebrity-filled event to benefit composer David Foster's charities. Tracey Gold was one of the others from the cast who flew in a private jet with me.

Several times I was asked to play at a celebrity tennis tournament at Las Hadas, an opulent resort in Mexico.

Probably the most memorable jaunt was when a friend and I traveled to England and France for a celebrity tennis tour to benefit charities sponsored by Fergie and Prince Albert for the Princess Grace Foundation in Monte Carlo. French Open champion Arancha Sanchez and I defeated Prince Albert and French Open champion Michael Chang in a knock-down, drag-out doubles tournament. (Not that I take much credit for the win.)

It was amazing to stay in palatial accommodations without paying a dime for them. In Monte Carlo, the view from my hotel room wasn't bad for a 17-year-old boy: directly over the bikini-clad French Riviera. My friend and I agreed that someone must have rounded up the most beautiful girls in Europe and placed them all on that beach.

We hobnobbed with the Prince at a gala, followed by a near all-nighter at a dance club. The gorgeous women in their 20s left me immobilized. I would have liked to dance, but . . . again . . . I was *immobilized*.

After the tournament and related events, we spent some time touring Italy and Switzerland.

On Location

The magical words for actors are "on location." Who doesn't want to work and vacation at the same time, all on someone else's dime?

Growing Pains was such a success that the network spent extra money to send us all to exotic locations. The costs for such undertakings were astronomical, considering the trips included the entire crew, as well as equipment. We did an episode on a cruise ship to Mexico and went to Hawaii twice. I enjoyed Hawaii so much that I went back two times on hiatus with friends.

The network then did something extremely unusual: They agreed to send the entire cast and crew to Paris and Barcelona for a two-part show.

The Gulf War had just begun and the President had restricted air travel for Americans in some parts of the world. Although Barcelona and Paris were not on the list, I was still very uneasy. I was concerned that our plane might be shot out of the sky by some crazy, American-hating terrorist. Under the circumstances, I didn't think it was wise to go on the trip.

I wished I wasn't such an integral part of the script so that they could write me out of the episode. I didn't want my apprehensions to affect so many people. I told the producers they should go on without me.

They, understandably, didn't want the Seaver family going on vacation without their son Mike. I was informed that the producers had spent $100,000 on pre-production trips already, spending tremendous time and effort finding the locations, hiring people, and so on. They'd even had special hats made that read "Barcelona or Bust." I didn't know what to do.

Finally, they sat me down and asked me point blank, "Are you going to get on the airplane and go to Barcelona? Yes or no?"

I swallowed the lump in my throat and said, "I don't think I can."

The producers looked at each other and said, "We're done." And everyone got up and left.

The whole thing was called off. One of the studio execs approached me and said, "Warner Bros. would never, ever put you in harm's way. If we didn't believe it was 100-percent safe, we wouldn't even suggest it."

I had put brakes on a freight train, bringing it to a screeching halt. I felt terrible. *Have I made the wrong decision here? Am I overreacting?*

All I knew was that our country was at war. It felt like we were an international target. Traveling on an American passenger plane over the Atlantic seemed not unlike riding atop an old mangy horse and trotting past a glue factory. It had nothing to do with a power play.

The producers didn't outwardly express anger, but I knew they were incredibly frustrated with me. I had shattered the excitement of a hundred people who wanted to work in a dream location.

Warner Bros. moved the episode to Catalina Island just off the coast of California, and did their best to make it look like Spain. It was a beautiful spot—but definitely not Paris or Barcelona.

My difficult choice reverberated through the industry. I was perceived as a big-headed little punk who thought he could tell the studio what they could and could not do.

Industry Events

I didn't like most industry events. I couldn't stand that kiss-kiss-hug-hug phoniness. Regardless, some shmoozing was mandatory—it came with the job. Promotion and publicity were essentials to the gig of celebrity, but they often made me feel like a zoo exhibit.

It wasn't so bad if I was in control of the environment, but if it meant wearing a suit and tie, hopping on a plane and showing up at some red carpet event with pretentious people, I couldn't get out of there fast enough. I was uneasy surrounded by people I didn't know. In general, I was incredibly shy and didn't like hanging out with strangers. Of course, certain people and circumstances could pull me out of my shell, but most of the time I could be found checking my watch to see when I could make my earliest escape.

I loathed Hollywood award shows like the Oscars, Grammys and Emmys—except for the time Chelsea and I went to the Emmy Awards in a limo and I did a pratfall on the red carpet, tumbling down the stairs in front of the paparazzi. While bystanders gasped in concern, Chelsea howled uncontrollably. (She swore it was one of the funniest things she'd ever seen.) Twenty minutes into the party, we were so much more interested in each other than in the award-show boast-fest that we snuck out the back door and had our driver take us to The Ivy, an irresistibly romantic restaurant in Beverly Hills.

Sixteenth Birthday

Mom suggested we throw a huge birthday bash for my sixteenth birthday, per the standard for child actors in the industry. That was the world we lived in back in the '80s. (Now, of course, Hollywood parents host blowouts for their children before they've even exited the womb.)

I chose a colorless theme. Everyone was instructed to wear black, white and silver. I dressed in the sparkliest silver outfit I could find—my wardrobe guy probably dug it out of a trunk marked "Garish"—and donned zebra-printed socks and fruity silver Tinkerbell slippers. The room was decorated with black, white and silver banners, balloons, linens and table decorations. A big ice sculpture sat on the cake table. A DJ spun Prince, George Michael and the Jacksons—Michael *and* Janet.

Mom was then on her umpteenth diet, and we decided the party would honor the culinary needs of everyone. We had food stations set up: Pritikin health food, Asian cuisine, spicy Mexican options and cheese-loaded Italian food. As an added joke, my dad set up exercise bicycles near the Pritikin corner.

The invitation list included everyone: junior high school friends, the cast of *Growing Pains* and their families, the crew and all of my relatives. Michael J. Fox came to toast me and give me some "big celebrity brother" advice. Photographers were invited as well. (Hey, if we were spending that kind of dough, we figured we'd take advantage of the photo op. It wasn't often that Mike Seaver and Alex P. Keaton were in the same space.)

The party went on late into the night. Maybe it was the positive energy or maybe I was on a sugar high, but I finally let my mullet down and got out on the dance floor. Someone snapped a photo while I was mid-Electric Slide, totally into it, fully enjoying myself.

Car Shows

I traveled all over the country making appearances at car shows. I guess the logic went that young girls would beg their dads to bring them and the promoters would get the sale of two admissions instead of one.

I'd show up in Salem, North Carolina, or Wichita, Kansas, or Wooster, Pennsylvania, along with 100,000 people and booths, food, games and rebuilt cars from the '50s, '60s and '70s. "Through the long dark winters, it gives these guys something to do," Dad explained. (Being a California boy, I never fully understood long winters. In L.A., it's cold when you have to throw on a hoodie.)

I agreed to do these shows because I didn't see any reason to say no, and they usually paid me good money. One time a promoter didn't have the cash, so he asked if he could give me a car as payment. I declined, since I'd recently bought my beloved, white Honda Prelude.

The line of girls was beyond unbelievable. I spent 10 seconds—max—with each girl saying, "Hi, how are you? How are you doing?" as I scribbled my name on a photo. I could sit for three hours straight signing autographs and there would still be a line as far as my eye could see.

Because we often took the red-eye flight after the car show in order to be at a mall opening by morning, we could get pretty tired. Once, Alan Thicke fell asleep in the middle of signing his name. *Alan Thiiiiii* . . .

Playboy Mansion

I received an invitation to the Playboy Mansion to attend a party that promised to be loaded with stars and hopping with bunnies (pun intended). At the time, Dad was beside himself. "Go, Kirk. You'll never get a chance to do this again! It's a once in a lifetime opportunity."

Mom shot Dad a dirty look and said, "Kirk, I don't want you to go. I don't think it's a good idea. It wouldn't be good for you to go, or for your career. If anybody takes a picture of you while you're there, even something very innocent is going to reflect badly on you." And then she started to cry.

Dad waved his hand dismissively. "Don't worry. Go. You'll have a great time."

"Kirk," Mom said. "I'd be hurt if you went. But make your own decision. If you aren't home by 6:00 after work, then I'll know you went." She turned on her heel and went to her room.

Dad winked. "Go, Baby Buck. Go for the both of us."

I had been thinking about the invitation before I brought it up to my parents. I, like my dad, figured it was a pretty amazing opportunity. But a part of me was intimidated. I was afraid of what might happen to me there. I knew I was young and naïve. What would I be getting myself into?

I trusted my mom as my manager enough to know that if she thought it was a bad idea, it probably was. And I trusted her as my mother.

Deep down inside, I didn't want to go. Really, I was in search of an excuse to bow out. So in typical teenage mode, I put it on her: "Well, if it means that much to you, then I won't go. Fine, Mom. Rob me of my fun."

I was home by 6:00, safe and sound.

Punk'd

I didn't get my driver's license until I was 17. I was just too busy to take driving lessons and to put in the practice hours. When I was finally legal, I bought a car. I loved my brand-new white Honda Prelude. I loved it the way a woman loves her firstborn.

One day on the way to work, I dropped it off at the shop to get a tune-up. Midway through the day's rehearsals, Mom ran up to me and said, "Kirk, you need to take this phone call." Her face looked not unlike it had when I told her about the invite to Hefner's party. I took the phone from her.

"I'm sorry, Mr. Cameron, but someone stole your car off the lot," a voice said. "You know, we just put it out there for a few minutes with the keys in it while we were shifting cars around. And it's gone. We've already notified the police."

I tried to pull it together. "Thank you for letting me know," I muttered.

A few hours later I got a call from the police. "Mr. Cameron, good news. We've gotten your car back. If you'd like to come pick it up . . ."

Mom took me over right away. I couldn't get my hands on my baby fast enough. The officer slowed my momentum by first asking for my autograph. *Give me a break! You've got to be kidding me*, I thought as I scratched *Best Wishes—Kirk Cameron* on the back side of a blank traffic ticket. Even law enforcement wanted a piece of me.

Outside the garage sat another guy, wearing grease-covered overalls.

"I'm Kirk Cameron. I'm here to pick up my car."

"Which one is it?"

I described it.

"Hey, guys!" he shouted into the darkness of the garage. "Haul out the Prelude."

A tow truck appeared through the garage door, carting what was left of my car. It had been stripped down to nothing but the frame. My stomach churned. I was horrified.

I began to walk around my shell of a car. One of the drivers handed me a tennis shoe that had been in my trunk. "This yours?"

I nodded numbly and took it from him.

As I inspected the car, I noticed something off, and went to whisper to my mom. "This isn't my car."

"What? Are you sure?"

"It's not my VIN number." How I knew my VIN number by heart is another mystery. I've said it before—I was an odd kid. It probably had something to do with learning to memorize things quickly for my acting career.

Just then, another car drove up: mine. Hanging out the windows were my dad and sisters. "You're on *TV's Bloopers and Practical Jokes*!" they yelled.

In today's terms, I had been punk'd. I'm just glad I didn't pull a Timberlake and break down in tears.

Fan Club

Right after *Growing Pains* premiered, I started getting fan mail. Eventually I was getting 10,000 fan letters a week, which added up to 120,000 letters every three months—almost a half million letters a year. (See? I know basic math.)

The mail truck showed up at our house and began unloading bins filled with the letters. At first, I read and answered each one—but that quickly became impossible. Then for a stretch of time, Mom took over the job. She read each letter and responded with a picture postcard.

But Mom already had a job as my manager. She enlisted the help of Grandma Jeanne and some church ladies to take on the Herculean task. Occasionally those sweet women came across blunt letters from men in prison, but mostly they received notes from young girls. Many included photos and other little gifts for me. A lot of packages arrived with stuffed animals. Grandma Jeanne donated these to the Children's Hospital. More than once, a pair of panties fell out of an envelope. Those were donated to the dumpster out back.

There were great letters about how much the girls loved Mike Seaver—or the entire Seaver family. Every so often a fan confused me with Todd Bridges from *Diff'rent Strokes*, but I appreciated the compliment on my beautiful ebony skin.

Some wrote sad stories about their struggles of being in abusive families and living very difficult lives. Many wrote of their dreams and wishes.

Mom wanted to be sure each received something in return, but eventually it was too costly, so she started a fan club. Kids could get a bunch of things for 10 bucks. (This was during the aforementioned *Kirk Cameron Pillowcase* heyday.)

For years, the ladies faithfully took care of the letters. Grandma Jeanne even became long-term friends with one of the girls when she felt a desire to respond to her letter. We relied on those ladies so much. Grandma Jeanne says it was a joy, but it still involved a lot of hard work, for which we were very grateful.

Celebrity Friends

This paragraph is pitifully short. Most of my friends were non-industry people. I vaguely knew Michael J. Fox and, of course, Leonardo DiCaprio got his start on our show—but we didn't hang very often. Sorry to disappoint you.

The Darker Side

There is a darker side to the lifestyle of the rich and famous. Making a lot of money puts you at risk of people taking advantage. I and some other cast members fell victim to such a scheme. My business manager stole over one-third of my total earnings.

I started out with a professional showbiz management firm. An employee named Walter was the go-to guy, a business advisor for my parents. When I got old enough, I stayed with him. He was a sweet man whom we trusted completely.

Walter wasn't qualified to invest money in the stock market, so he suggested I hire a firm that could handle investments. This firm charged several thousand dollars a month to manage my account, which seemed to be an awful lot of money for what they were doing.

Walter contacted me one day and said, "These guys are ripping you off. The truth is, you don't need their services. I'm basically doing all the work anyway. These guys are just collecting a check. Dump 'em."

I was so appreciative of his advice that I gave Walter a raise.

He slowly set up a system that gave him check writing authority on my account. We neglected to set up any kind of checks and balances with him—certainly no one suspected that our trusted advisor would do anything shady.

Walter bought diamonds, furs and watches for his boyfriend. They took extravagant trips to Hawaii.

The party ended one day when Walter's secretary saw a cancelled check in the trashcan and turned it over to me. "I think you need to check on this," she said graciously.

How can this be? This is Walter, our family friend. We trusted him with everything. In hindsight, it was obvious that the guy had problems, that he was on the edge. He was skittish, filled with anxiety and ready to jump. He got to the point where he wouldn't look me in the eye, often resembling a cornered squirrel.

When we saw him we'd say, "Wow! Business must be really good for you. You wear Italian-made suits. Your boyfriend wears a black mink coat, Rolex watches and silk jumpsuits. You must be great with money."

He was great, all right. Great at snowing me.

I took the check to a man named Gavin de Becker, *the* authority on celebrity protection. "How do I get this money back?" I asked.

Gavin, as usual, asked a lot of probing questions. He felt Walter might be at high risk for fleeing the country. He said we needed to find a way to corner Walter away from his home, without arousing suspicion.

It would have been a highly intense situation for anyone—let alone a teenager. Gavin's plan made me nervous. I was emotionally rattled and could barely make the phone call to Walter. "Walter, I'm having some problems on the set and I really need to talk to someone. My parents are on that Alaska cruise with everyone. I'm here by myself and I need to talk to a friend. I'm hanging out at this hotel, can you meet me here?"

He agreed and I met him in the lobby. "Walter," I said, "I decided I needed to get away and rented a room. We can go there to talk privately."

He agreed. We got on the elevator and I noticed how fidgety he looked. That made two of us. When we got to the room and opened the door, Gavin and three of his henchmen were there with open black briefcases filled with written and photographic evidence.

Walter's face fell. He turned to look at me and said, "I protected you from everyone except myself." And then he confessed.

Later he told me that when he heard my voice on the phone he knew what was up. "I knew I was walking to my own demise, walking into a trap. I felt so horrible that I was doing this to you. I was sick and I couldn't stop myself. I needed someone to stop me."

He did protect me from everyone else. He was always trying to protect me from people who tried to take my money in other areas, people who wanted me to invest in their businesses or ventures. He saved me pennies while costing me millions.

Because of Walter's confession, the trial was quick. He went to prison.

My Crib

Most young people work for years to build up enough of a nest egg to buy a home. One of the lifestyle perks was that I bought my own house when I was 18 years old.

I found this really cool house in Simi Valley, California, in a hippie-biker area called Santa Susanna Knolls. The place was rustic and unconventional and, as legend had it, built with drug money. An eight-foot barbed-wire fence surrounded the property and the windows were set high in the stone walls so that outsiders couldn't see in. It had a bell tower that housed an old school bell with a rope that hung into the kitchen—probably to signal when police or shipments arrived.

I lived in my own Swiss Family Robinson digs, built on seven levels against a steep hillside. It was so in sync with nature. It had patios resting on boulders on the hillside. It had wood burning stoves in the bedroom and one in the den.

The top level above the main house was a guest quarters with a little loft bed, wood-burning stove, sink, toilet and a smokin' view of Simi Valley. Outside the guest quarters was a big bathtub. Yes, a white porcelain bathtub plumbed up with hot water, perched outside on the rocks to take baths in the breeze. There was nothing like it.

I didn't live there long because I met and married a girl who preferred a quaint condo by the lake. Sadly, my cool mountain cabin burned down not long after I moved out.

Chapter 12

Fans Gone Wild

A fan is a strange thing to have. I'm not talking about whirling blades that provide relief in the heat. I'm referring to enthusiastic admirers, ardent devotees. Who was I to have *fans*—throngs of people who wanted a piece of me?

Thanks to my job, the Camerons could no longer have Friday night dinners at Mission Burrito without being swamped with attention. I had to stop going with my friends to Disneyland and Six Flags Magic Mountain. I could wear sunglasses and a baseball hat, but it only took a glimpse of my crooked smile or curly hair for someone to recognize me.

I eventually created a disguise I wore in public. I sported a mustache, boots, round sunglasses, slick hair and ratty jeans supported by a belt with a large buckle. I walked with a swagger, speaking to my friends (who called me "Dale Olson") in a bad Southern twang. It was like a reality show where the makeover had gone tragically, painfully awry. *I* looked like a fresh-faced, wannabe cowhand. *It* looked like a Halloween costume.

Once "Dale" swaggered his way through a mall that proved a bit too humid for the mustache. It slipped until one side drooped over my lips like a caterpillar falling from a branch. I high-tailed it out of the mall with one finger on my 'stache, wondering if people were commenting on the frenzied, nose-picking cowboy. The only thing worse would have been for them to recognize me and ask, "Why is Kirk Cameron dressed as a hillbilly? What some people will do for attention . . ."

I wondered why I couldn't just go about my business and have folks leave me alone. The truth is, I didn't understand things from their perspective. Now, years later, I have better insight into the eagerness of fans. I realize they are just very excited to meet someone they never thought they would.

I was a fan myself. I was a huge *Happy Days* fan back in the day. As a family, we watched it every single night. There was no cooler man on the planet than The Fonz. You remember: the guy who could walk into a room, snap his fingers and have every girl in the place instantly on his arm ready to snuggle up and slow dance.

I remember the first time I met Henry Winkler. I was invited to a fundraiser to benefit a hospital that specialized in helping burned children. The event was at Mr. Winkler's house. Once I arrived, I scanned the crowd, looking intently for the man in the black leather jacket, with the perfectly combed hair and a girl attached to his hip. Suddenly I was interrupted by a very short, soft-spoken Jewish man in a three-piece suit. He looked at me very sincerely, and said in a voice as soft as bunny fur, "Thank you for coming today, Kirk. My name is Henry Winkler."

I about fell over. *The Fonz in a suit?!* My hero with gray hair and no blue jeans or black leather cool? When I got over the initial shock of the physical discrepancy, I slipped into that star-struck fog in which time appears to stand still. Your brain doesn't work, you say things you later lament, your words don't make sense and your adrenalin turns your ears red and makes your hands sweat. Quite simply, you are *beyond* excited.

It happened to me three times in my teenage years. The other two times were when I met Brooke Shields and Arnold Schwarzenegger.

So I understand how people feel when they walk down the street and see Mike Seaver. They're genuinely excited to meet someone they grew up with, someone who made them laugh in the cozy safety of their living room or den.

As I matured, I learned to really appreciate my fans. I enjoyed talking with people from all walks of life. It was cool hearing that *Growing Pains* comforted them and brought joy into their lives. So many found a surrogate family in the Seavers—the family they wished they'd had. Some just identified with another happy family, as I had watching *The Brady Bunch*. I especially enjoyed hearing stories from guys who permed their hair like mine hoping to attract the ladies, or patterned their pubescent pranks after Mike Seaver's and got into just as much trouble as he did. What these young guys forgot was that I had 12 professional writers to get me out of the trouble they got me into.

I didn't mind giving fans my time—when I had it to give. After all, it was their support that kept *Growing Pains* on the air. But it *was* challenging when each meal eaten in a restaurant was interrupted every few minutes by an excited person wanting to chat and ask for an autograph. Their comments were rarely brief.

So I developed my own ways of dealing with the never-ending interruption: I discovered that if I made eye contact, people saw it as an invitation to come talk to me—so I stopped looking at people. I'm sure many thought I was unfriendly and aloof, but there came a point when I could no longer please everyone and retain any part of life to call my own. I wasn't the type of guy who enjoyed disappointing people, but my Just Say No policy started to apply to more than just drugs.

If fans came to my table at a restaurant, I tried the polite approach. Sometimes I signed the autographs and let them say what they wanted to say. Other times, when I was in the middle of an intense or important conversation, I might say, "I'd be happy to take a picture with you as soon as I'm finished with my meal."

Some took the hint, others snapped at me. One time while enjoying a family reunion at an inn in Geneseo, New York, my mouth was entirely occupied by the Surf 'n' Turf special. An impatient fan didn't want to wait for her autograph, so she blurted loud enough for all to hear, "Boy, you sure are a lot funnier on TV. And you're a much bigger slob when you eat." Comments like that just sucked the joy out of lunch.

I was amazed at the people who thought I was horribly impolite for not accommodating them *that instant*—and said so. They never considered themselves rude for interrupting *my* meal to talk.

That's the irony to me. People say, "I don't want to interrupt you, but . . ." followed by complete, utter interruption. They *do* want to interrupt you; they just don't want you to get ticked with them for doing so. If you, on the other hand, kindly ask them to wait until your meal is over, they go off on you! I often wonder how *they* would feel if a stranger approached them, asked them to put down their fork, sign a napkin, smile with food stuck in their teeth for a picture to be posted on the Internet, and then launch into a walk down memory lane while the food turns stone cold.

I stopped trying to run quick errands. A five-minute trip to the grocery store turned into an hour when a gaggle of fans all wanted "just a minute of my time." Sure, if only one person wanted a minute of my time, it wouldn't be an issue. But when 20 fans each wanted a minute (which was *never* a minute) and I needed to be somewhere in 10, it simply wasn't possible.

I trained myself to be oblivious to the gawking of those around me. Being followed every step through a store could be very unnerving, so I had to block out everything around me or feel more self-conscious than I already did. The staring alone could ruin my day if I paid too much attention to it.

Once I was on an ocean rafting adventure in Hawaii with friends. Two young ladies from England apparently sat with their backs to the gorgeous scenery, staring at me the entire trip. Even though they couldn't have been more than four feet away, I had no idea they were ogling me until one of my buddies mentioned it. I was busy staring at the beauty of Kauai's wild north coast, and they were busy staring at me. Talk about misplaced priorities. Those poor girls stepped onto land having no idea what they had missed. If I hadn't ignored their stares, I, too, would have missed the splendor of the island—and had the pleasure stolen from my trip.

Fever Pitch

Fans have cut locks of my hair, ripped off pieces of my clothing and appeared uninvited at my home. One girl, after standing in line to get an autograph, literally passed out the moment she got to speak to me. Even worse, she fell off the stage and broke her leg.

My sisters love to tell stories about their experiences when fans mobbed me.

At car shows, a limousine was usually used to get me safely through the crowds. After one appearance, I crawled into the limo along with my mother and sisters. On my way into the car, a girl shoved a handful of rose petals into my jacket pocket. As usual, excited girls jumped up and down, squealed and screamed my name. I thought I'd do something sweet and toss the rose petals to the fans as we drove away—something for them to keep as mementos.

I rolled down the tinted window a few inches and scattered the petals as the car moved slowly through the crowd.

"Kirk!" Mom shouted. "What do you think you are doing?!"

Her warning was too late. The moment the window opened, girls shoved their little hands through the gap, trying to grab me.

Mom frantically tried to bat their hands away in order to roll up the window—only she succeeded in trapping my arm. We drove off, my arm pinched between the window and the frame.

Just Say No

Parades brought out the craziest moments. At a Just Say No parade in Chicago, Tracey Gold and I were on top of a tower as emcees for the parade. The story is more interesting from the point of view of those below, so I'll let my sister Bridgette tell it:

The plan was for this limo to show up behind the tower. Kirk and Tracey would come down and get inside this getaway car. But somehow, the word got out. When Mom and I got to the car, there were gobs of girls screaming, waving, surrounding the base of the tower. Hundreds of them. Mom and I were staring up at Kirk, who was stuck. Every time he tried to climb down, the girls grabbed at his legs.

"What are we going to do?" Mom asked the security guard.

"Get inside and wait," he told us. "We'll have to snatch Kirk off the tower and shove him in."

Mom and I couldn't see through the tinted windows until suddenly, the door flew open and someone literally threw Kirk inside.

We didn't go anywhere. The car rocked and bounced as the hysterical girls swarmed all over it, pounding on the windows, shrieking and screaming, "Kirk, Kirk, Kirk. We love you, Kirk!" Some of the girls sobbed.

I couldn't believe it. *For my brother?* I was thinkin'. *Get over it.*

The driver honked the horn. The girls at the front of the car startled a little but didn't leave. He laid on the horn and they still didn't move. He tried inching forward, but that didn't work either.

Mom and I huddled together, scared of these maniac girls. I was afraid one was going to break a window.

Finally the driver jumped out of the car and started screaming, "Get out of the way!"

Somehow between the guards and the shouting limo driver, we were able to make a very slow getaway.

Bad Manners

It's nerve-racking to have the entire world looking for your flaws. My sister Candace's first kiss of her life was on television. Magazines reported every normal, fluctuating weight pattern and evaluated them in detail. Tracey Gold developed anorexia, in part as a result of the never-ending pressures and critical attention to her appearance. My every teenage insecurity is now available on DVD and for download on AOL.

When some people watch a show long enough, they become very bold when they approach an actor in person. They feel connected on some level because they spent 30 minutes a week with their "television friends," and this sometimes leads to a sense of entitlement—which, in turn, leads to very bad manners.

I'm dumbfounded at the things fans have said to me, presumably without thinking. When I was going through puberty they liked to walk up and say, "Wow, nice zits" or "You're a lot skinnier than you are on the show." For a guy who worked out in the gym two hours a day, five days a week, *skinny* was not the physique I was going for.

Now, at 37 years old, I get, "You were sooooo good-looking when you were younger" or "Holy cow! I guess I'm not the only one going gray." Sometimes I want to ask if these are the first comments they make to close friends. Probably not. Perhaps they are just so startled when they unexpectedly see a famous person that they say the first thing that pops into their heads.

I often feel like Homer Simpson: It's as though people don't see me as a real human being. It's like they're talking to a cartoon character they've always known and I've gone and changed the drawing on them.

Paparazzi

It was one thing to have fans interrupt every meal, but paparazzi were entirely different animals: scavengers who took invasion of privacy to a whole new level.

The bread and butter for these people is to get the best photo of a celebrity and sell it to one of many tabloids or magazines. It was bad in the '80s, and it has only intensified now in the world of TMZ.com, rags like *OK!* and *In Touch*, and 24-hour cable celebrity coverage. Americans' appetite for this stuff seems insatiable.

Back then, guys with cameras seemed to appear in packs—seemingly out of thin air—ready to blind me with light. I had no idea how they knew my plans. It felt as if someone was tipping them off to my every move. When I showed up for a personal event that I thought no one knew about, paparazzi were waiting for my arrival. They pushed to get close, and their intensity almost brought them to blows.

It's not that I fault them for wanting to put food on their table, but there was no sense of social grace. Were they raised by flocks of crows?

One exception was Roger. He was always polite, requesting a photo shot instead of demanding one. And before he took the picture, he'd always ask, "How's your mom? How's your dad? How are your sisters?" As a result, I happily gave him any picture he wanted.

Because of his consistent courteous approach, after a while I'd see him in the crowd and say to the security guards, "Hey, this is my friend Roger. I'd like him to come on this side of the ropes so he can get all the pictures he needs." I'd take him aside in front of all the other photo hounds and give him all the pictures he wanted. The rest of the paparazzi were like vultures, trying to get a piece of me to sell to the highest bidder.

It didn't happen often, but sometimes I could outsmart them and have fun slipping through the paparazzi unnoticed.

Once, my parents and I were at a celebrity event. I didn't feel like dealing with photographers that day, so Dad and I went into a bathroom and switched clothes, hats and glasses. We got on our bicycles and rode in different directions. We looked a lot alike, so it worked. I made my escape while Dad had a blast leading the snapping fish upstream.

I don't know if anyone had more fun than my dad when he pulled off the disguise and saw disappointment flash across their faces.

After I started living alone, and then after Chelsea and I married, I pulled every drape and closed every blind when the sun went down. Paparazzi hid in bushes and peered through my windows to get a shot. I wanted to be able to privately dance with my wife on our patio overlooking Lake Calabasas. I wanted to enjoy the gorgeous, warm California nights. But I felt so exposed to those enormously powerful lenses. When Chelsea and I adopted our first son, someone took a photo of me carrying him in his infant seat *in the private courtyard approaching our condo*. That was probably the first time I was truly angry at the intrusion of my privacy.

It's funny about human nature: Everyone wants to be noticed, to be seen and appreciated. But when you get too much of it, you want to go back to what you had before—invisibility.

Most people can choose when to step into the spotlight and when to step out. But for a child star, there is no stepping out of the spotlight. It follows you no matter where you are, no matter how inconspicuous you wish to be.

And then one day, for most child actors, the spotlight abruptly shuts off. Just as suddenly as it shone, it flickers to dark.

Chapter 13

Growing Dangers

Mike Seaver experienced light-hearted growing pains, but for a while my real life played out like a gritty episode of *Hill Street Blues*.

One day, a couple of police officers showed up at my set trailer and asked to speak with me privately. My mom invited them in, and the four of us sat at the small, built-in dining table.

"Who's your partner?" the taller officer asked me.

I had no idea what he was asking. *Does he think I'm gay? Is he referring to my character's best friend, Boner?* I was completely baffled by the question.

The older officer held up a picture of me and a good-looking guy in his 20s. We stood side by side with the *Growing Pains* set behind us. "Tell us what you know about this man. We know you work with him."

They were so forceful in their accusation.

"He looks familiar," Mom said, squinting at the photo.

"Yeah," I said. "I remember him. He came to the set awhile back. He said his brother is dying of cancer in Canada. He's a fan and wanted to take a picture with me to send to his brother."

"What else are you guys involved in?" the officer pushed.

I could tell they meant business.

"Nothing, I swear."

I was confused, replaying in my head the occasion of meeting this guy. I'd taken photos with thousands of people, but I remembered that this guy had been on the set a few times. I figured he was friends with a cast or crew member. I recalled the day he told me the story of his brother and how much it would mean to him to have that picture. He didn't have a camera, so I ran around and found one and then had Jeremy take our picture. He came back a few days later to pick up the photo. I really hadn't had much contact with him.

"How long have you been in business with this guy?" the officers asked again.

I shook my head. "I don't know . . . I'm not in business with anybody. What kind of business do you mean?"

They scrutinized every move I made. I rubbed my sweaty hands on my parachute pants and swallowed hard. I felt guilty, even though I knew I wasn't.

"Are you dealing? Got something going on the side?"

I was incredulous. "What? Are you kidding me? I've never even smoked a cigarette. I'm the Just Say No kid!"

"Kids lead double lives—it's not unfathomable," one of the officers quipped.

"That's not possible," my mom said indignantly.

"You can ask anyone on the cast," my voice cracked. It wasn't nearly as cute as when Mike Seaver's voice popped—I just sounded guiltier and guiltier. I tried to convince them I didn't know this guy beyond the little contact I'd had with him on the set.

"We did ask around," an officer said. "But we still had to ask you."

Mom stared at the picture, her mind churning.

The officer tapped the picture with his finger. "So you don't know anything about what he did with this photo?"

I shook my head. The policemen went on to explain that the guy had doctored up our photo to make it look like an official ABC publicity shot. Pulling out a yellow notepad, the officer said, "This man used this photo to lure a boy about your age into his car. He told the kid he worked with you and could take him to meet you." The policeman swallowed and looked at my mother before he spoke. "Instead, he raped the boy at gunpoint."

I was overwhelmed. I'd never heard of something so sick and twisted. And to have my name attached in any way to such a horrifying crime repulsed me.

My mother broke the silence and gasped. "I know where I've seen him! He came to our house one day asking for Kirk, saying they had met at the gym." She rubbed her temples fearfully. "Kirk wasn't home. I can't believe it! I invited him into our house to write his message on a piece of paper."

The officers looked at each other. I started to figure it out. *This man had been trying to get me.* I broke into a flop sweat.

"We'd like your help in catching him. We need Kirk's cooperation."

"How?" Mom asked.

"We need him as bait."

"Absolutely not," my mother shook her head emphatically. "I will not put my son at risk. I won't have my son in that kind of danger."

Seeking Protection

On hearing what had happened, Alan Thicke recommended we see Gavin de Becker, an expert in dealing with celebrity stalkers. My parents and I went to see him in his office.

Driving down an alley, we followed instructions that led us to a high, nondescript wall. I pressed the button on the wall and a voice spoke. "May I help you?"

"We're here to see Mr. de Becker," Mom said.

"Do you have an appointment?"

"Yes. For Kirk Cameron."

A steel door crept open, revealing the front door of a house. We walked through the courtyard and saw a planter to our right. We pushed on it, as instructed, and a door opened to another set of locked glass doors. It was very *Inspector Gadget.*

When we finally entered the inner sanctuary of the office of Mr. de Becker, I expected a menacing man with a booming voice, petting a cat with his silver claw. Instead, we found a small, thin man named Gavin who looked like an accountant. But we had been told that when it came to celebrity protection, he was the best in the business.

We spent several hours with Mr. de Becker. We gave him the police report and told him everything we knew. He asked probing questions before giving his assessment of the threat level. He profiled the type of stalker we were dealing with and outlined typical behavioral patterns.

We left with a list of things we had to do, including changing our phone number and having the original number rerouted, obtaining a P.O. box so that no one would have our home address, and hiring an armed guard to sit in a car outside our house around the clock.

From that day on, an armored limousine arrived to take me to work. Each day I stepped into the bulletproof car, knowing that men had scanned the area to insure my safety. Mr. de Becker taught me to walk through crowds with my head down. Fewer people recognizing me insured a better chance of not getting hurt. My parents had an electric security gate installed around the house so that no one could approach the front door. Dad installed motion-detector security lights on the driveway that led to my apartment in the back.

I felt like I was living a bad dream.

Sting Operation

I didn't know until much later that the police stayed in continual contact with my parents, repeatedly asking them to allow me to participate in a sting operation.

My parents resisted, until it sank in that another child could be hurt by the man.

"Without Kirk there is no way we can contact this man without him becoming suspicious," a detective told them.

"Can you keep him safe?" Dad asked.

"We can't guarantee it, but we will do everything we can to protect him. He's our first priority."

With my parents' permission, I agreed to cooperate in luring the man back to the set.

My hands shook as I dialed his number. "Hey, it's Kirk," I said, trying to keep my voice calm and normal. "I'd like to have you come back to the set and hang out after the taping tonight." I hyped it up a little. "I'll give you a backstage pass and a special parking spot. Afterward, you can join me and the rest of the cast for dinner."

It was, perhaps, the finest performance of my career.

The police told very few people what was planned for that night. The fewer who knew, the greater the chances they could catch the guy. No one in the cast or crew knew what would happen right outside the huge stage doors.

The police locked me in a darkened dressing room with a guard outside the door. I wasn't allowed to leave until the whole bust was over—not that I would have wanted to. Just sitting there, waiting for him to show up, was scary enough. *What if the officers don't see him and he finds me?* I asked myself. *What if he comes in the trailer and we get locked in together?*

I watched through a small window as undercover police replaced the regular studio security men with their own officers. Within moments, everything looked normal. An undercover cop dressed in a cap and overalls pushed a broom like a janitor. Another, dressed as a set dresser, drove around in a studio golf cart.

Right on time, a light-blue Oldsmobile convertible stopped at the guard hut. The undercover agent playing the guard chatted cordially with him for a few moments, and then the stalker reached for his parking pass and slid it onto the dashboard. He pulled into a parking space reserved for "Special Guests."

Wearing a white T-shirt and jeans, he opened the car door and stepped out. At that second, a sea of men spun toward him, guns drawn.

"Drop to the ground, *now!*" they shouted.

The man collapsed on the asphalt.

"Lace your fingers and put your hands behind your head!"

Within seconds, the officers had seized the man and locked him in handcuffs. The pedophile was thrown into the back of a car and hauled off to jail.

New Security Measures

After that horrific incident, the studio decided to install metal detectors through which the fans and audience would have to pass. The whole situation had so freaked me out that I wanted to test the new machines to see if they really worked, so I went into the Craft Services kitchen and got the biggest butcher knife I could find. I slipped it up my jacket sleeve.

When I got to the detectors, I smiled at the security guards. "Hey, boys. How's it going?"

"Fine, Mr. Cameron," one replied as I breezed through the metal detector. It didn't even make a peep.

On the other side, I turned around and said, "Oh, guys . . . I forgot to give you this."

I pulled the butcher knife from my sleeve.

They gasped and said unrepeatable things. Shocked and embarrassed, they couldn't believe I had gotten through.

I laughed nervously, hardly reassured. "Yeah . . . I feel much safer now."

Chapter 14

Teen Atheist

*I*s *there more? Have I peaked? Is this it?*

Just as everything in life seemed to be going my way, I started to ask myself deep, probing questions.

My father's financial dreams and visions of independence were what emotionally motivated him for the long haul in life, and by those standards, I had already arrived. I was a bit miffed. I was 17 and had already surpassed what most people hoped to achieve in a lifetime.

The disturbing part was that it all felt very empty to me, kind of like biting into the big chocolate Easter bunny: It looks great on the outside, then *pop!*—hollow on the inside. Or like looking forward your whole life to meeting Santa Claus and then finding out that he's just an out-of-work fat man in a polyester suit.

I felt that I would have traded it all for something else, but what the "else" was, I had no idea. It was kind of depressing. I always thought being rich and famous would make me infinitely happy, but it didn't. *Weird.*

What did I have left to look forward to? More money? More fame? More admiration? Was the rest of my life gonna be more of the same? Was the American dream of health, wealth and prosperity a sham—as phony and make-believe as a Hollywood façade?

There was this gnawing in my gut, insisting that something was missing. *There must be more to life than this,* I reasoned. *Is there a God? Is there a heaven? Have I been wrong about these things?* If there wasn't anything but the here and now, then nothing mattered but having a good time. *Let's eat, drink and party hard till the lights go out. If death is the end of the road and life is about getting what I've already got, then let's get busy living life wide open till we die.*

Peggy Lee's 1969 hit "Is That All There Is?" sums up what I was feeling in 1987: "If that's all there is, my friends, then let's keep dancing, let's break out the booze and have a ball . . ."[1] Where was this song when I needed it? Maybe it was on the flip side of a record Dad had glued together.

While every other teenager wondered how they could bag a babe every Friday night, I had no idea why I was preoccupied with loftier questions. I had no idea what a "soul" was, but I was getting the sense that if I had one, mine obviously lacked something. At first, I figured I could forget about my questions by masking them with a relationship with a woman. If I could just find the right one, maybe *that* would satisfy me and fill the emptiness I felt inside.

Where would I find such a girl? I needed someone who wanted to get to know the real me and wasn't just excited about the status of being with Kirk Cameron, Teen Heartthrob. Where would I discover someone not caught up in the superficial? L.A. didn't seem likely. Perhaps Alaska. Or East India. Some place where women were too busy surviving to watch situation comedies.

There Is No God

The idea of "God" felt very silly to me. I was conditioned to believe in atheism. It was what I had always been taught in school as a kid. My science teacher didn't believe in God and anyone with half a brain was an atheist, too—or so I thought. It just seemed so rational, so smart. I was an individual—a free thinker. It was like, *See? I'm not some stupid, vapid TV star. I've thought things through, and I say, "There is no God."*

I had friends who had faith in God and spoke of "Him" as the most significant part of their lives. That troubled me. I felt sorry for these small-minded plebeians, who were obviously victims of religious brainwashing. I didn't hold it against them; I just pitied them a bit. As far as

I was concerned they could worship Bigfoot, as long as they didn't impose their fairy-tale beliefs and archaic morality on me.

But the big questions wouldn't leave me alone. *How did we get here? Does it really matter how I live my life? Does anyone really care? Could there be a God? What will happen to me when I die?*

I must have been asking my spiritual questions out loud, because a set designer gave me a book she promised would change my life. It was called *YOU*. The title appealed to my self-centered psyche. It explained that I was God and that the power of the universe resided within me, and that I just needed to recognize my potential and embrace it.

I read it, but in the end I couldn't buy into that philosophy. I had trouble making rice that didn't clump together, let alone create my own universe. Besides, if *I* was God, then why didn't I know that I was God? Why did it take a paperback to clue me in?

I knew the reason I was "important" was simply because I was on a TV show that made a lot of money for a lot of people. It was all about what I did and what I could do for them. As soon as teenage girls were done with me, my agent would be done with me. And so would Mary Hart and John Tesh. And so would *People* and *TV Guide*.

My "power" was as thin as wet crepe paper.

I did take a few ideas away from that self-help book. I figured that if belief in a god helps one feel better about life and get through the day, it doesn't matter whether it's real or not, or who he/she/it is or what one calls god. I decided to experiment with that philosophy to see how a "god belief" would make me feel. I liked the concept that a god could be anything I wanted it to be. I was like the writers in the *Growing Pains* writers' room: Just as they pulled stories and characters out of thin air, I could do the same in my creation of "god."

I thought my god should have a name, and figured that *what* you call god is not important. I had always liked the name "Mark." It had a nice hard *K* at the end of it. So just for yuks, I named my god Mark.

Havin' Church

Around that time, I met a very pretty girl on the set. She was one of a set of triplets, which, I know, sounds like a story begging to be turned into an episode: *Mike tries to date triplets simultaneously, but learns a valuable lesson about deceit.*

But no, I just dated one of the sisters. She was a sweet girl who eventually invited me to join her family for a trip to church. To be perfectly honest, I didn't want to go. But I accepted the invitation—not because I was interested in religion, but because I didn't want to offend her family.

It was a big church. The head honcho was a man named Chuck Swindoll. He had a booming voice and spoke with authority. I listened as he read from a Bible, which I thought was nothing more than a book full of rules designed to suck the fun out of life. This pastor began to share the biblical description of God in terms I had never heard before, in a way that grabbed my attention and dazzled my intellect.

He spoke of God's omnipotence: God is *all-powerful*. He talked about God's omniscience: He is *all-knowing*. And he addressed God's holiness: He is *morally perfect* and, therefore, He alone defines what is good.

I spent a lot of time thinking about those things.

I knew that while Earth seems huge when you're in an airplane, the truth is, it's just a spec in comparison to the sun. And the sun is a relatively small star in our huge galaxy. The big ones are many times larger and occupy billions of other galaxies in the universe. The universe is so huge that we have not yet found the outer edges. If God created all this and sustains life on Earth—the only place that has life as far as we know—then how powerful and intelligent must He be? The thought was mind-boggling to me.

I later heard a scientist explain that Earth is basically a large rock being hurled thousands of miles per hour around a ball of fire we call the sun. If the Earth were to break from its orbit just a fraction, we would either burn up or freeze to death. "If no one is in charge of this whole thing, we're in trouble," he said.

Then he added, "If Someone *is* in charge of this whole thing . . . we're in trouble."

That Sunday morning at church with my friend's family, I thought, *If God is real and eternal, and made everything out of nothing as the Bible says, it makes sense that He also knows every piece of His creation intimately. That means there is nothing He does not know. God knows not only what's at the outer edges of time and space, He also knows who shot JFK, and the details of the secret love lives of the fleas on the back of every cat. That means He also knows every thought and every intention of my heart.*

The most sobering statement I heard that day was that God was "holy," absolutely good. He abhors evil, which meant that I might be on the receiving end of some anger and wrath. After all, my secret thought life and private actions betrayed my image as the squeaky clean role model everyone believed me to be. Apparently, I was a "sinner." The Bible made it clear there is a stubborn, selfish streak that runs deep in the heart of every person. It shows up when we lie, steal, fail to love God, dishonor our parents, are greedy, hateful, and so on.

Dr. Swindoll spoke about heaven and hell, and immediately followed that up with talk of God's mercy and love. He explained that God, in His kindness, provided a way for sinners to be forgiven of their sins, washed clean, changed and made new. He spoke about the value of grace, repentance and faith.

I was blown away. I felt like someone had unloaded a theological dump truck on my head. These were not the words of the irrational, big-haired, crazy loons I had seen on religious television, swindling Social Security money from senior citizens desperate for a miracle. Dr. Swindoll wasn't promising health, wealth and prosperity in exchange for a donation to his ministry, but rather freedom from God's wrath and a relationship with the Creator of all things. Swindoll appeared totally sincere in his beliefs and genuinely concerned about the welfare of his hearers.

I left the church with a long list of questions. My date's father did his best to answer them and then turned the tables on me, asking me pointed questions that caused me to examine my own long-held atheistic beliefs. He then suggested that I read Josh McDowell's book *More than a Carpenter*, which turned out to be the first intelligent essay I'd ever read about God. Up until then, God had seemed like nothing more than a mythical creature lumped in with a different trinity: the Easter bunny, Santa Claus and the Tooth Fairy.

I continued visiting that church, seeking an answer to the huge question of God's existence. To me, it became the most important question I could answer. *If there is a God, a Creator, a supreme Being who created all of this, the implications are HUGE!* The existence of God would certainly answer my questions about where I came from, what I was supposed to be doing here and where I was going when I died. But the enormity of the task overwhelmed me. *How do I go about this? Where do I start?*

I began reading the writings of men whose intellect I respected. To my shock, I found that many historical heroes believed in God, such as Albert Einstein, Sir Isaac Newton, Copernicus, and others. I later found that even champions of atheism such as English philosopher Anthony Flew had converted to belief in God, partly based on Einstein's conclusion that a supreme Being must exist.

To be fair, I also researched the other side of the debate. To my surprise, I found that even Charles Darwin, the man who popularized the theory of "molecules-to-man" evolution operated within a framework of belief in God.

Despite my confident denial of the existence of God, I began to seriously question if I could be wrong. I often parked on the top of a hill at night, gazing out the window of my car, in awe of the countless stars in the sky. I tried to comprehend not only how far away the stars were, but how they got there in the first place. I sat for hours contemplating how this tiny, fragile planet we live on could be so perfectly balanced that it supports such a vast array of life forms, from huge elephants and whales to tiny hummingbirds and insects. I wondered what laughter is and why it feels so good to laugh with a friend. Even though I couldn't see love, I knew it was a priceless treasure and wondered if anyone or anything had created it. Why were sunsets beautiful? Why did the birth of a baby make adults cry with joy? I had so many questions that begged a meaningful answer, but for so long, I wasn't willing to critically examine my atheistic beliefs. I had been blinded by my own pride. I had been unwilling to look up and ask God for the answers.

Slowly but surely, as I considered the hard facts, I began to lose my faith in atheism. From my study of science, I was committed to having intellectual and ethical integrity, and adhering to the scientific process. That meant that I would follow the evidence wherever it led, regardless of my own personal bias. As I continued to uncover simple, rational, logical evidence for the existence of a higher power, I could not, in good conscience, hold to my denial of God. I did the unbelievable: I opened my mind to the possibility of a powerful, intelligent Designer.

Back to the Pews

A few more times to church had me listening carefully to the pastor, contemplating every word. One of the most compelling things about the God of the Bible, I found, was that He valued me for who I was.

I learned I had value simply because God had made me in His image.

But I had chosen to willfully reject God and turn from Him. That had great negative value in the eternal equation.

God knew the core of me—the totality of every thought, emotion and action—and cared about the *real* me. Surrounded by a world of superficiality, this was a new and humbling concept. God knew me—the Kirk He had made—with every hope and dream, every fault and flaw. I would not be the celebrity in this relationship.

A month after my first visit to her church, I dropped my friend off at her acting class in the San Fernando Valley. As I pulled away, something flashed through my mind: *I'm part of the ultimate statistic: 10 out of 10 people die. I'm going to die one day. If it were to happen in the next 10 minutes—if I were to get in a car accident and die—what would happen to me?* The thought overwhelmed me. I felt smaller than a speck of sand.

I pulled over to the curb and turned off the engine. *If there is a God and a heaven, there's no reason He should let me in,* I told myself. I had gotten past the intellectual barrier to God, but I knew there was a bigger stumbling block that stood between me and my Maker. It was not intellectual, but moral.

I knew that because of my prideful attitude and the way I had intentionally ignored—even *denied* God—especially in light of the good things He had given me, I wouldn't go to heaven. Instead of loving God, I had mocked the Giver of all that was precious to me. Deep in my gut, I knew my arrogance and selfishness were an offense to God. Without ever having read the Bible, I intuitively knew that I was a walking violation of the first and greatest commandment: I had failed to give the Creator due honor and respect.

I was sure that if I died on Van Nuys Boulevard that day, God would be perfectly justified to exclude me from heaven and instead give me whatever I deserved.

I wanted to pray, but didn't know how. Closing my eyes—hoping no one was watching—I muttered, "God, if You're there, will You please show me? If You're real, I *need* to know. And would You please forgive me for the things I've done that are wrong? I don't want to join a religious cult or believe in a fairy tale, but if You're there . . . I want You to change me into the person You want me to be."

Tears came to my eyes. Goosebumps formed on my arms. I felt that I was unworthy of talking to God.

When I opened my eyes, I didn't see a vision of Jesus on the windshield. The Holy Spirit didn't rush in through the air conditioning vents. Nothing weird. I just sat there thinking that I had just spoken to the *Creator of the universe* and that He had heard me.

Little did I know that those feeble and honest moments of seeking God in my sports car would forever change my life.

Note

1. Jerry Leiber and Mike Stoller, "Is That All There Is?" (Nashville, TN: ATV Tunes LLC).

Chapter 15

Having an Opinion

1988

I lifted the receiver of the brown desk phone. *I do not want to do this.*

I was stuck in a no-win situation any way you looked at it. Pacing my dressing room in 1988 (see chapter 2), I weighed my options and didn't like either of them. I would either go along with what the producers wanted, or I had to tell them how I felt and stand by my convictions. Both options would be painful.

I wanted to be on good terms with everyone on *Growing Pains*, and I knew the phone call I was about to make would make that almost impossible. I wrapped the curly phone cord around my finger and punched in the executive producers' office extension.

"Hey, how's it goin'?"

"Great, Kirk."

"Hey," I said, trying not to sound nervous. "I have a concern about one of the scenes and I wondered if you guys could help me out with this."

His voice tightened. "Sure. Let's talk about it."

"Thanks. When do you want me to come down?"

"Now would be good."

I hung up the phone, knowing by his tone that the following conversation would only get more awkward.

I drove the half-mile to the producers' building on Warner Bros. Ranch, turning down my Amy Grant cassette. Even her soothing sound couldn't calm my anxiety. I pulled into one of the available spaces out-side the administrative bungalows, took a deep breath and went in.

I walked past the office cubicles in the musty, stucco building. A few production assistants exchanged curious looks: *Why is Kirk Cam-eron in our building?*

I knocked on the producers' door and entered at their prompt. Sitting on the sofa, surrounded by awards and framed *Variety* maga-zines, we engaged in painful, drawn-out small talk.

"So, how're things going?" I asked.

"Good, Kirk. How's rehearsal?"

"It's going well."

"Alan behaving himself?"

I smiled. "Never."

Everyone laughed politely, until one producer took the lead. "So, Kirk . . . what's up?"

I cracked my knuckles, buying myself two more seconds of time.

"It's about the opening scene," I said, referring to the part we had been rehearsing that day. It called for Mike to open the show in bed next to a beautiful girl. He was to roll over and say, "What's your name again?" Later it would be revealed that he was only acting out one of his mother Maggie's vivid nightmares.

Dream sequence or not, I didn't like the idea of viewers seeing Mike so casually in bed with a woman.

"Why are you even in here?" one of the writers pushed.

I didn't know if he meant "Why do you even have a problem with this?" or "Who do you think you are, punk? Let us write the show" or "Why don't you just tell us what you want us to do, because we're just going to have to do what you say, anyway."

I didn't bother to ask. "Because I'm concerned. I know I have a re-sponsibility as a role model, and parents trust us to be able to watch this show with their kids. I just don't want to do anything that would give kids the idea that I have a casual attitude about sleeping around."

They looked at me like they'd eaten some bad ham.

I was a 17-year-old kid talking to 40-ish men, but I wasn't stupid. I knew how my comments came across. I sounded as though I was implying that my moral standards were higher than theirs.

"I'm not asking for you to can the whole scene," I hedged. "I'm just asking if there's another way we can do this so that I'm not uncomfortable and can give it 100 percent."

They glanced at each other, looking less like comedy writers and more like reporters covering a gruesome strangulation case.

"I'm not trying to create some set of standards *you* need to live by," I went on. "I'm saying that for *me*, this crosses the line in my conscience . . . and since I'm the guy who has to get up there and do this in front of millions of people, I don't want to do it."

"We'll talk about it and let you know," one of them said, with a sigh.

I stood. I had articulated my feelings as respectfully as I knew how. I muttered, "Have a great day," though I'm sure no one heard me.

Power Play

I was *not* looking to pick a fight to show everybody who was boss, contrary to almost everyone's belief. I was trying to be respectful and cooperative—to work the creative process with them as a team. Believe me: It wasn't worth the agony to fight over these things if I was simply trying to throw my weight around.

I find it amazing that actors can throw scripts against the wall, refuse to say lines, demand more money, show up two hours late for work and you never hear about it—but the minute an actor has issues with script content based on moral convictions, it gets blown out of proportion on the set and in the press.

Supervising producer Joey Scott tried to help me understand what the folks behind the show were trying to do. He explained that the writers wanted to be edgier now that Mike was older. They wanted to show a kid growing up and exploring the issues that develop during adolescent years. The writers wanted to be real about sex, drinking and drugs. "If Mike Seaver is a popular kid—not a bad kid, but edgy—he gets into mischief and doesn't always do the right thing at first," Joey said. "Kirk, Mike is a better guy if he is tempted, goes right to the edge and backs off, doing right by the end of the show. In the long run, he makes the better choice."

"Joey, I totally agree with you." I said. "I have no problem with that. You're misunderstanding me. I have issues with only the details of a couple specific scenes, not the entire character of Mike Seaver. Why is that so hard to understand?"

John Tracy, our director, pulled me aside and we talked. He found a compromise for the scene. I was fine with the changes. I agreed to do it and the show came off fine.

Over time, however, I became more introspective and even pulled away a bit from the cast. My former M.O. was to be a prankster—I had no problem joining in on off-color jokes or rude stories flying around the set.

But things started to change when my conscience began to kick in. The cast and crew didn't understand what was going on inside of me—only that I was withdrawn and antisocial. The once fun-loving prankster was now oh-so-serious. I became very guarded, careful and deliberate—not nearly as carefree—because I was trying not to make mistakes with regard to morality.

People thought I had another agenda than I did. They felt I went off the deep end or that I was flexing my celebrity power—or both. I never wanted to do that. I never wanted to be seen as an egotistical idiot. The reality is that I was struggling to take steps of integrity, trying to do the right thing.

Wardrobe Malfunction

Generally speaking, I only spoke up over issues that *my* character faced.

In one episode, Mike's girlfriend, Kate, was doing a photo shoot for a swimsuit calendar. There were about a dozen girls who were wearing . . . well, let's just say they weren't dressed for a trip to the North Pole. I watched as a dozen very scantily clad girls became the subject of rude comments and the gawking of a few salivating writers and crew members. (Some of these girls had obviously augmented body parts that were barely contained by the skimpy suits.)

I thought of the families who would be watching at home.

I rehearsed the scene all week with the girls and thought the sexy-factor was over the top for an 8 o'clock family show. I didn't ask that the girls dress in 1940s bloomers and bathing caps, but I also didn't feel that our show needed to resemble the Victoria's Secret catwalk. I spoke up.

Rather than understanding my motive to protect our show's family-friendly reputation and the dignity of the actresses in the scene, some people got very upset with me.

"Now Kirk's making wardrobe decisions for other cast members?"

"Where is this heading? Is he going to tell us what *we* can and can't say or what I can and can't wear? Is he going to make decisions for my character? C'mon, producers . . . nip this in the bud."

The last thing I wanted was to be anyone's personal censor. The reality is that I was struggling to take steps of integrity and trying to do the right thing. Unfortunately, when I made a move, it affected a lot of people. I was in an unnatural position. Most 17-year-olds aren't put in a position of power that can influence an entire company—but in a sense, that's where I was.

It would have been far easier to go with the flow. I would have made a lot more money—not just on *Growing Pains*, but for offers after the show ended—if I had played the game. It's not easy to stand up for what you believe. I learned that at a very young age.

Setting the Story Straight

Contrary to popular gossip, I had nothing to do with the firing of Julie McCullough as my TV girlfriend because she posed for *Playboy* magazine. But don't take my word for it. According to Dan Guntzelman, the head show-runner for *Growing Pains*: "The truth is, Julie was let go because Mike being in a committed relationship was a dead end—he was, after all, an immature imp who was ill-equipped to deal with a grownup world on all levels. That's where the conflict and comedy came from: The maturity to have and maintain a lasting relationship fought against this. . . . Julie was to play the part of Mike's first serious relationship—

the first time he was swept up in something larger than himself, but she was never intended to be his mate for life, even the life of the series."

Producer Mike Sullivan confirms Dan's comments: "It was a guest star role; she wasn't hired as a series regular. There was never any intention of the Mike character being married or in a permanent romantic relationship."

Some people today question why *Growing Pains* ended or why the producers quit the show. Some say it was because I was difficult to work with due to my personal convictions. Again, Dan Guntzelman: "As important as Kirk's struggles were to him, they were not the primary focus for me. Most successful sitcoms have a life of five, six or seven years, then the pressures to end it start to mount: Actors want to move on, the show gets top heavy. (How many executive producers does it take to screw in a light bulb? About 10 in the fifth year of a series.) A family sitcom has an even greater incentive. (Kids grow up and there goes the family.) Leaving *Growing Pains* was the logical thing to do. Also, selfishly, coming off a hit show made you 'hot.' It was the perfect time for me to get a new deal and try to 'do it again.'"

On the set of the *Growing Pains* reunion movie, I approached the producers and said, "Hey, I wanna let you know . . . a lot of years have gone by. I've thought a lot about what happened during those years and I know that I could have handled those situations more graciously than I did when I was 17. We had a lot of great years together and I hope you can forgive me for any frustration I caused you."

One producer replied, "We're sorry. We probably didn't handle it the best way, either. We really could have tried to help you out here instead of just hammering you every time you asked for something."

I talked to the cast as well. As time gave us a better perspective, I think we all were able to look at the situation with more understanding. I'm glad we had that time of reunion and reconciliation.

We enjoyed shooting another reunion flick in 2004, *Growing Pains: Return of the Seavers*, which Joanna directed. The whole cast assembled to shoot a special feature for the *Growing Pains* DVD set, in which we enjoyed a marshmallow roast and a fun walk down Seaver memory lane, reminiscing about all the fun times we shared. We saw each other recently at

Alan's ranch outside of Santa Barbara to celebrate his son's birthday. And Jeremy occasionally comes over to our house to prepare some of his famous gourmet dinners for our family.

Chapter 16

Lips that Tingle

One fateful day, I decided to stop by the set of *Full House* to show the little sis some support. My sisters had always cheered on my career, and I wanted to show Candace some big brotherly love in return. Maybe I could give her a few pointers about comedy. (She's gonna love reading that.)

That day, I'm sure Dave Coulier was nearby doing a celebrity impersonation. Maybe Bob Saget was telling an off-color joke. Perhaps one of the Olsen twins needed a diaper change.

All I remember was a willowy brunette with caramel-colored eyes and beautiful lips that framed her stunning smile. Her long hair fell around her face and barely swept her shoulders, and she had a gorgeous figure.

Chelsea Noble was guest-starring on *Full House*. She approached me and asked, "You're Candace's brother, right?"

It was strange, yet cool, to be referred to that way. For once, it wasn't "Oh-my-gosh-it's-Kirk-Cameron-can-you-sign-my-Trapper-Keeper?!" This was a mature, sophisticated woman a few years my senior.

She asked me to take a picture with her wheelchair-bound friend who was visiting from New York. I happily agreed, and talked with the girl in the wheelchair for a while.

Later that night, Mom remarked, "Do you remember that girl you met, Chelsea? If I could pick a girl for you to marry one day, it would be someone like her. As beautiful as she is, she's even more beautiful on the inside."

Chelsea

I loved Kirk's mom, Barbara, just from knowing her briefly on the *Full House* set. She was easy to talk to—very different from the stereotypical "stage moms."

Then when I met Kirk, I thought, *Wow, what a nice guy.* He sat and talked with my friend for a while. I could tell it made him happy to make her happy. I left thinking, *What a caring guy.*

A few weeks later, I was in the process of getting ready to move back to New York. My agent had suggested I go to an audition for *Growing Pains.* "You might make some money before you go back home."

When I hesitated he added, "You never know . . ."

It was rush hour—and anyone who has ever driven in L.A. traffic knows that you really don't want to be out there if you don't have to. I almost didn't go on the audition, but my agent had a point: I needed the job.

I walked into the audition room. The casting director took one look at me and said, "Are you sure you're here for *this* role? You're not the right type."

Sure enough, the role was for a "character"—a larger-than-life, wise-cracking secretary. Why was *I* called in for this?

Inside, I fumed. *I drove all that way, and for what?*

The director shrugged and said, "Just read for it anyway since you're here."

That comment took the edge off the interview. I thought, *Ah, they're just humoring me. Whatever.* I had never been so casual about a read. I kicked back and had fun reading the role.

When I got home I called my agent and told him it had been a big, fat waste of time—mine and theirs.

"Oh yeah," he quipped, "you really blew it. They just called and offered you a different role—the role of Kate, a girl in Mike's acting class. It's coming up in a couple weeks. Congrats."

When I showed up on the set of *Growing Pains*, it was really awkward stepping into the world of such an established cast. The director took me aside and said, "Okay, this is what we expect from guest stars.

We expect you to be here on time. The regular cast shows up a little later. That's just the way it is. It's your job to get in the groove of what we've got going here."

When Kirk showed up, I was a bit surprised. I knew *of* Kirk Cameron, but I'd sort of forgotten what show he was on. I know that sounds implausible, considering how famous he was. But I really wasn't a big TV watcher. I just remembered him as Candace's sweet older brother.

Kirk

When I saw Chelsea on the set, I immediately remembered she was the same girl I had met on *Full House*. How could I forget? I'd been overwhelmed by her beauty and her smile.

I approached Chelsea and without thinking gave her a kiss on both cheeks. Inside I cringed that I'd done the phony Hollywood *kiss-kiss* thing. *That wasn't me! What am I doing?* It was the first of many uncharacteristic moves I'd make in trying to impress this girl.

From the start, I slipped into familiar awkward territory. Though we worked long hours together that week, I kept a reasonable, professional attitude and distance.

One day, sitting to the side of the set, Chelsea wore cowboy boots, jeans and a white cotton shirt. Though her hair was long and flowing, I could see a headset on her ears. Around her neck hung a necklace with a cross made of sapphires. As I looked at that cross I thought, *Could she be a Christian? No way. She's too beautiful.* I thought girls were either beautiful or Christian—not both.

I walked up to her and asked what she was listening to.

Chelsea

I thought, *There's no way this guy is going to know this band.* I was listening to a CD by the Christian rock group Petra.

To my astonishment, he said he knew them. And then he just kinda smiled and asked if I was a Christian.

Stunned, I said, "Yeah, are you?"

"Yeah."

It was the weirdest moment. I just didn't expect it. It was great to have that kind of connection with him—but then again, there are so many kinds of "Christians," so I wasn't really sure what that meant to him.

Kirk

We got talking about music, our faith and our families. I just loved talking to her. I didn't want it to end.

I had a thousand butterflies, but tried to keep my growing feelings hidden from this girl who seemed way out of my league. I figured that if she was available, Alan would probably make a move on her. He had a lot of luck with the ladies. Besides, Chelsea was a few years older than me and she probably thought of me as "just a kid."

Thank God she didn't.

Instead, Chelsea and I hit it off. We had so much in common, including a deep and growing love for God. We had fun on the stage, but always looked forward to the time behind the scenes when we could get to know each other better. It was a great two weeks.

But I figured that after the show, I'd never see her again.

Chelsea

After the second episode, the producers called me to the green room in a building across from the sound stage. *Had I done something wrong?*

"You know, Chelsea," a producer said, "we really like the chemistry between you and Kirk. We don't see that very often and we'd like to explore it more. How would you feel about coming back for 13 more episodes?"

I was taken aback, flattered. The only thing holding me back was a job offer in New York. I had booked a dramatic TV pilot playing a law student. I really thought drama was the direction I needed to pursue, and the part in the pilot sounded like the perfect role for me. I also really missed my home state of New York and was dying to get back. I didn't say any of that to the producers. I thanked them for the offer and promised to seriously think about it.

My agent, naturally, leaned toward me staying. Thirteen episodes would be a lot better financially for me than one pilot. Those come and go, and most never make it to air.

He said, "Chelsea, you haven't done much comedy. Why don't you just do the 13 episodes—it'll look fantastic on your résumé."

I agonized over the decision.

Eventually I agreed with my agent that it would be good to go back to *Growing Pains* and get this valuable experience.

It was one of the best decisions of my life.

Kirk

Passion and fashion didn't mix—at least, not in my case.

Remembering that Chelsea wore Levis and cowboy boots to the set on more than one occasion, I figured that must be a look she was into. So I tried to impress her by wearing a green cotton work shirt and boots I'd inherited from the film *Listen to Me*. Walking in those clunky heels, I looked like a teen ranger with a spur stuck in his boxers.

She didn't seem to think anything of it.

I learned from our conversations that Chelsea liked skiing. The next day I wore a vest with ski tags and lift tickets pinned to the chest.

Everyone in the cast stared at me, dumbstruck.

"Hittin' the slopes after work?"

"Hey, Kirk. You forgot your goggles."

I shrugged. "Oh. It was a little nippy when I got up this morning. Thought I'd come prepared." *It's Los Angeles . . . and you're indoors, dumbnut,* I thought to myself.

They knew something was up, but Chelsea didn't know me well enough to catch on. She must have thought I was the type of guy who really enjoyed dressing in themes.

I eventually thought dressing *GQ* was the way to go. (Most guys go through a *GQ* stage. It usually follows the doused-in-aftershave stage.) I scoured the men's couture magazine for the latest styles. The next day I showed up on set looking like the guy on the cover, wearing a white suit shirt, skinny tie, shorts and Birkenstocks. I was 50% Don Johnson,

40% golfer, 10% hippie. I didn't pull off the look. It's a wonder Chelsea even spoke to me.

I reached deep within and found my inner-Mike Seaver, finally working up the nerve to call her after work.

"Hey, how's it goin'?" I asked. "Any chance you wanna join me and a couple friends for mud pie at Red Robin? We're just planning on hangin' out . . . I thought, maybe if you're bored . . ."

When she said, "Sure!" I freaked. I frantically called every friend in my Rolodex because I'd made the whole thing up: There were no plans to have mud pie at Red Robin. And now that I needed there to be plans, no one I knew in Southern California could spare one hour for pie.

Chelsea was already on her way. I drove down to meet her, stewing. I had wanted a friendly, no-pressure situation, and now it would be just the two of us.

It was a cold night, and we sat outside on the patio wrapped in warm coats. (That ski jacket didn't look so bad now.) I thought it was romantic, sharing a desert. (Yes, according to the "fun facts" in *BOP* magazine, I was a reported germaphobe. Didn't matter with Chelsea. I wouldn't so much as share a slice of pizza with the woman who had given me life, but this fascinating beauty was a completely different case. *Someone this beautiful doesn't have germs*, I told myself.)

As we talked, I only wanted to kiss her. I admit it.

Chelsea

He seemed nervous and somewhat awkward that evening, but 100-percent genuine. He had no pretension, which was incredibly refreshing.

I liked him from the start. I found myself thinking about him when I left work.

When my friends heard I was working on *Growing Pains*, the common question was, "What's Kirk Cameron like?"

"You'd be so surprised," I answered. He seemed like somebody I could have grown up with on the East Coast. It kind of floored me. He didn't strike me as a self-absorbed, Hollywood teen idol.

He was really sweet and down to earth, and kind of shy. And his mouth! I was crazy about his mouth. He had the greatest crooked smile— I would just watch him as he talked to me. Sometimes I wouldn't even hear what he was saying. I was just thinking, *I would love to kiss that mouth.*

Kirk

When Chelsea came back for 13 weeks, I about flipped when I read the script titled "Triangle." There, in the middle of the episode, I was supposed to kiss her.

What are the writers thinking? I'm going to kill 'em. They're going to blow my cover!

I tried to play it calm and cool during the initial table reading, though my heart thumped like the bass to an MC Hammer hit. In the script, Kate and Mike are in an acting class together, performing a scene from a play. Mike is playing George, who says to Kate's Virginia, "Don't cry, I'll be back" before planting a big kiss on her lips.

Mike had kissed a lot of pretty girls on the show, but none were even close to Chelsea in beauty and spirit. All I could think of was what she would think of me after I kissed her on taping night.

I had major angst over this. *She probably has preconceived ideas that this teen idol must be Mister Smooth—Don Juan.* With my overactive imagination, I could see her backing up after the kiss, startled, wiping her mouth with the back of her hand and saying, "What are you, a chicken? Do you have a beak for lips?"

During rehearsals, I played it cool by waving my hand and saying, "And then we kiss and I leave." I hoped to pull off an unaffected, breezy attitude that gave the impression I wasn't fazed in the least.

I never actually kissed her in four days of rehearsing the scene. It seemed to go unnoticed until a cameraman said, "I need to see how the kiss shot frames up, Kirk."

He was on to me.

When it came time to kiss Chelsea in front of the audience, I knew I had to come up with something to take the edge off. I purged the First Aid kit in the prop department, looking for the right balm. I needed this to work, so I lubed up my mouth like lip gloss on a cheerleader's senior photo.

Perfect.

Chelsea

When it came to the part where he kisses me, he *really* kissed me. It just wasn't what I expected. This was no half-hearted screen kiss.

I noticed, though, that some of the crew smirked and held back laughter. What was so funny?

The kiss was nice, but I was surprised how moist Kirk's lips were.

I licked my lips to get the wetness off. Within seconds, my entire mouth—my tongue, my gums, my teeth—were utterly numb. The camera pushed in on me, waiting for my line.

"My mouth is, like, paralyzed," was all I could say. "What's going on? I can't feel a thing."

Kirk turned to the audience and shrugged. "What can I say? That's the effect I have on girls," he cracked. "My kisses are electrifying."

Kirk

I had smeared Anbesol, a numbing gel for teething babies, on my lips. And I had put a *lot* on to make sure it worked. It did. It also broke the ice and made it easier for me to kiss her.

I think director John Tracy gave me a hand by insisting we do the scene over and over. "Uh, Kirk . . . bad focus here. Can you do it one more time for me?"

"Happy to take one for the team," I grinned.

Chelsea

That memorable scene made me see how fun he was. I loved his sense of humor. After that, Kirk and I began seeing each other frequently.

Kirk

I still didn't think this amazing girl would be interested in a date alone with me. When Michael W. Smith came to the Universal Amphitheater on the Go West, Young Man Tour, it was the perfect chance to ask Chelsea to go with me and my buddies.

She agreed. And this time I didn't have to call anyone. I really did plan to go with some friends.

We met at Mom and Dad's house. After introductions and small talk, I opened the door for Chelsea to sit in the back seat with my buddy's date and jumped into the passenger seat to ride up front. At this point, I was sure she only saw us as friends and I didn't want to make her uncomfortable.

Dad shook his head in disbelief. I could hear him saying, "Son, are you crazy? Have I not raised you right? *Why* are you not sitting with that gorgeous girl in the back?"

I realize I was 19, but I was too anxious to be alone with her. Being that close would be awkward. I wouldn't know what to say or where to look. How would I play it cool without being obvious about my feelings? *Do I cross my arms? Fold my hands in my lap? Can a guy sit with hands in his pants pockets? No, that looks ridiculous!*

I chose the safe route and, like a doofus, left my date alone in the back.

Chelsea

Although we had spent quite a bit of time together on and off the set, we hadn't really been dating. I wasn't exactly sure where the relationship was headed, but it definitely felt like we had romantic potential.

One night, after dinner, the two of us sat in his parents' living room. He reclined on the couch, clear across the room from me. I was sitting next to the fireplace.

"I wanted to tell you that I've really loved spending time with you," Kirk finally said, after staring at me for a bit.

"I've enjoyed it, too."

"Well, uh, hey, I just wanna . . . I gotta tell you something. The more time I spend with you, the more time I want to spend with you. And I think I'm . . . falling in love with you, which is not good if you're not feeling the same way. So if you're not, tell me now. I'll get over it and put it out of my mind."

I was relieved that he'd said it first.

"I feel the same way," I said.

Kirk had the ability to make me feel like I was 12—his words and the way he said them made me blush. He wasn't a suave charmer—the guy sat on the opposite side of the room (when he wasn't leaving me in the backseat of a car!). It's that he was so sincere. He didn't ever seem to put on an act for me. He let me see the real him, and that's who I was falling in love with.

We sat there looking at each other, thinking, *I am so happy right now.*

Kirk

I kissed her goodnight at the front door of my parents' house before she left. It was our first *real* kiss.

Walking her out to the car, I waved as she drove off. My casual stride to the front door switched to mad whooping and hollering once inside the house.

I ran around the place like a crazy man, probably leaving tread marks on the walls.

Chapter 17

A Sticky Wedding

We didn't announce our romance to the world, but it was pretty obvious. When Chelsea walked onto the set, a smile appeared on my face that made me a dead ringer for Happy the Dwarf.

I had found everything I ever wanted in a woman. She was beautiful—inside and out. She had very strong values of her own. She loved her family. She loved God. She wasn't impressed or overly interested in my celebrity, but rather, wanted to get to know the real me.

The funny thing was, *I* had a hard time knowing who I was at that time. I had spent my entire life listening to directions from other people. From the time I was nine, my existence was written, produced and directed by others. I needed to figure out who I was. Chelsea helped me to do that.

The tabloids, however, had another take on our relationship.

Older Vixen Robs the Cradle:
Growing Pains Cast Fears for Kirk's Life!

Oh, the hysteria. For a time, the media had found their angle. Chelsea, being a few years older, was the best story the press could concoct. I suppose it was a better headline than "Wholesome Kirk Cameron Dates Even Wholesomer Chelsea Noble!"

Chelsea didn't bat an eye at the coverage. She found a way to laugh at what was said about her, even when one magazine said things like

"She whipped her brown mane around like Shahrazad's veil, capturing Kirk with her smoky brown eyes. Some would even say she was a Svengali."

Chelsea

I couldn't fight things people believed, so I didn't even try.

From the start, Kirk never seemed young to me. He seemed older than many people my age, because of his life experience. He was living on his own and he was working a professional job. I was just out of college, so compared to my college friends, he was a mature guy. He seemed so much more serious and surefooted than the guys my age. I never felt the age difference, not at all.

Of course, if he had been older than me, no one would have said boo.

Kirk

Not long after I sat by the fire and unleashed my true feelings to Chelsea, Valentine's Day was upon us. Though February 14 is a manufactured, Hallmark holiday, I wanted it to be unforgettable for Chelsea.

I put a blindfold on her eyes and put her in a limousine. It was about 5 o'clock in the evening. The driver drove around a little to disorient her before pulling up in front of my house. Then he opened the door for her, helped her out and took off the blindfold.

Chelsea

I was a bit startled. A man in a tuxedo, looking much like a maitre d', waited for us at the bottom of the long flight of stairs leading up the hill to Kirk's guest house. He gave a little bow. "Good evening, Miss. It's good to have you here."

Tiny fairy lights twinkled up the hill, lighting the path along the stone stairway.

The man opened the door to the guest house. I gasped.

Fresh flowers in an enormous wreath framed the huge picture window that looked out over Simi Valley. Candles were lit, transforming a simple room into something elegant and terribly romantic.

We were seated at a table with a linen cloth and handed a menu. Kirk had hired someone to cook a delicious four-course meal.

I was overwhelmed. This had obviously taken a good deal of planning and effort. And it had been orchestrated especially for *me*.

The evening was magical.

When we had finished our meal, Kirk escorted me to the bottom of the stairs where the limousine waited to take me home. We said goodbye. When I arrived home, Kirk was there waiting for me . . . *in my apartment!* It might have been a sweet, romantic moment, except that I had decided earlier in the day that it was time to do a little spring-cleaning—I had literally dumped every drawer of clothes all over the apartment so I could sort through them.

I was mortified.

Kirk

In early April, Chelsea decided she wanted to go home and see her parents in Cheektowaga, New York. She was very close to her family and planned to stay for a couple of weeks.

Not even a day into her trip, I felt as if my insides had been ripped out. I went home to hang out and Bridgette was there.

"Hey, Bridgette, come here and look." I took her to the back of my car and pulled out Chelsea's jacket. "It smells like her," I moaned. I inhaled deeply, her perfumed scent filling my nostrils.

"Don't let the paparazzi cameras catch you making that face," Bridgette laughed.

"I miss her *so* much."

Bridgette, who had seen one too many Molly Ringwald flicks, switched into sappy mode: "Kirk, you must run. *Go to her.*"

"What?"

"Get on a plane," she answered, with the unwavering conviction only a teenage girl can muster. "You must tell her how you feel. Before time runs out."

"I'll do it!"

I called Chelsea's parents (who I had never met) to be sure it was alright with them for me to come. Her father gave the okay, so I bought a ticket, threw some clothes in a suitcase and hopped the next plane out.

Chelsea

One day, my dad popped into the room and said, "Let's go to the Asa Ransom House for dinner. I've got my mad money. Let's make an evening of it."

I loved the Asa Ransom House, an inn located near the home I grew up in. At dinner, Dad and Mom asked questions about Kirk. They wanted to know everything about him. He was a little sketchy in their eyes, due to the fact he was an L.A. actor. Though they were skeptical, my parents trusted me. After all, I had lived in New York City alone for two years and had proved to make mostly good decisions.

In the middle of dinner, the waiter approached our table. "Ma'am, you have a phone call."

I felt so important. *A phone call in a restaurant? Is it my agent? Has he booked me a big job?*

"Hi, sweetie," said a familiar voice on the line.

"Kirk?"

"I don't want to keep you. I just wanted you to know I'm thinking of you and missing you very much."

"That is so sweet, Kirk. Thank you." After a couple minutes of unabashed flirtation, I hung up. My parents seemed impressed with Kirk's thoughtful call. Maybe this actor-guy was worth their daughter's time after all.

A waitress interrupted our conversation. "Miss, the gentleman by the fireplace wanted me to give this to you." She held out a long-stemmed rose.

"Dad!" I hissed. "What am I going to do? I'm *so* embarrassed." I reached back to retrieve my flower to find Kirk, holding a bouquet of roses. He had secretly arranged the whole thing with my dad. *Be still, my heart . . .*

Kirk

I stayed for the next two weeks, getting to know her dad, mom and brother. It was a great time of going from complete strangers to friends. Having seen what kind of family Chelsea had, I flew back to L.A. even more impressed with her.

Only a week or two after our trip, Chelsea got a call from her brother: "You've got to get home *now*. Dad is dying."

Chelsea called me, barely able to breathe, sobbing. I immediately booked a flight to New York and we got there before her father passed away.

When my sister had pushed me to fly to New York, there was a lot more going on than a romantic movie storyline. I believe the hand of God was at work in that spontaneous decision. Chelsea's dad was one of the most important people in her life—she says he was "one of the loves of her life." It would have hurt her beyond belief if I had not gotten to know this man who meant so much to her. And I enjoyed the privilege of spending two weeks with him.

During the summer hiatus from *Growing Pains*, I spent another month with her family at their lake cottage, getting to know Chelsea's extended family. By early fall, I began asking myself, *Is Chelsea the one?*

I followed that up with, *Can you picture your life without her?*

The answer was obvious: *No! I don't want to go a day of my life without her!*

I had always said I wouldn't get married until I was at least 21, and now at 19, I was giving it serious consideration. Was I too young? Most advised me to wait: "Don't give up your youth," they said. "Play the field. There's a lot of women out there. Haven't you heard? You're *Kirk Cameron!*"

Yet marriage never seemed like a crazy move to me. It felt right—that it was the next, obvious step in making our relationship permanent. I didn't want to ever let Chelsea go.

Through reading the Bible, I was learning more and more about God's design for marriage. According to divine design, marriage is a covenant, not a contract. A contract can be broken, but a covenant is forever. When marriage is just a contract, you will focus on your rights; when it is a covenant, you will focus on your responsibility. If you see marriage as a contract, you look for loopholes; when you realize it's a covenant, you learn to stay committed for life. Contracts are written on paper and based on mistrust—which explains why you put it in writing. (A lawyer advised Chelsea and me to sign a pre-nup, just in case things didn't work out. We refused.) A covenant, on the other hand, is a verbal promise based entirely on faith and commitment.

Many Hollywood couples split before the ice sculpture has thawed. You wonder why they even bother.

The following October, about a year after our first kiss by the fireplace, I bought a diamond for Chelsea. I had the setting modeled after the classic ring Tiffany made famous. It was perfect. I slipped the black velvet box into the inside breast pocket of a sport coat that hung in my closet. Every day, I made sure it was still there, checking before I left for work and again when I got home. I lived this OCD routine for two months, waiting for the right moment.

I brought my parents and sisters with me to spend Christmas in Rochester, New York, as guests of Chelsea's family. There, I took Chelsea's mother and brother aside to quietly ask permission to marry Chelsea. They both gave their consent.

Chelsea

I thought that if Kirk was going to propose, it would be on Christmas while both families were together—but it didn't happen. I think Kirk's mom was disappointed.

On December 30, Kirk and I shared a date at the Asa Ransom House (the same restaurant where Kirk had surprised me with the flowers) to exchange one more set of Christmas gifts. Snow floated down outside our window throughout dinner. Slowly the patrons left, until we were the last ones there. After our dessert plates had been cleared, Kirk gave me a small wrapped gift. I tore away the wrapping paper to find a heart-shaped, white music box. I opened it and stared at a beautiful diamond ring nestled in the center of a red velvet pillow.

Kirk slid to one knee. "Chelsea, will you marry me?"

I soaked in the moment and through tears said, "Yes."

Kirk

Just then, I saw a flash outside the window behind our table. Someone had captured our private moment on film. While I felt a bit violated, I shrugged it off and decided not to care. What could I do about it, anyway?

I had everything I wanted. I had Chelsea, and she was more than enough.

Back on the set, tension was as thick as military-grade nerve gas. My requests for changes had left many people angry. Some did their best not to speak with me. It didn't help that I had ostracized myself from them as well. While not all the cast members were openly at odds with me, others were—and it was very uncomfortable.

Animosity at work was one thing, but now that I was going to get married, I questioned what to do. *Should I invite my TV family—the Seavers—to the wedding?* If I did, I would also feel obliged to invite the producers, as well as some of the writers and members of the crew. I wanted things to be as they had been during our early seasons. But truthfully, it wasn't the same anymore. Even worse, I think some saw Chelsea as part of the problem—which I know really hurt her. She knew that she had nothing to do with the conflict.

I didn't want their presence at my wedding to be phony. I didn't want to be preoccupied with people who had resolved to have grudges against me. I envisioned the day we got married as the happiest day of our lives.

When I asked Chelsea about it, she said, "That decision is totally up to you."

I kept thinking, *They're so mad at me. They don't even like me. I don't think they'd even want to come. And the last thing I'd want is for them to feel they have to come out of obligation . . . or to put on a happy face for the inevitable press.*

I really felt badly that things were how they were. I didn't want them to be that way. I cared a lot about each of them. Not inviting the cast and crew wasn't about getting even. There was nothing to get even about. I was sure they weren't truly happy for us, which didn't exactly put them at the top of our guest list. I didn't see the point in inviting rain on our wedding day.

After many weeks of inner turmoil, I made a decision. Considering all the circumstances and feelings involved, I decided to keep our wedding day quiet and very private.

Chelsea

Almost every girl dreams of the perfect wedding. I was not one of those girls. I viewed our wedding as just that: *our* wedding. It was about Kirk and me, so whether things went "right" or "wrong" didn't matter because to me there was no right or wrong. (Which is a good thing, because my bridesmaid's flowers were absolutely hideous.)

We planned to marry in the small old chapel in Buffalo where my parents had gotten married. The old chapel didn't have any air conditioning, and we chose to get married on July 20, 1991—a day that was 90 degrees and 90-percent humidity. Even that was okay, because the wedding was perfect.

A woman designed an old-fashioned dress for me: long sleeves with real heirloom hooks and eyes from the neck to below the waist and from elbow to wrist. The dress was so beautiful—though I was 45 minutes late to my wedding because of those crazy hooks! At one point, I was resigned to walk down the aisle with the back of my dress split in the shape of a capital *V*. My bridesmaids, dripping with sweat, worked so hard to help me, like animated mice in Disney's *Cinderella*.

The chapel was beautiful in its simplicity; we had no need for elaborate decorations. I carried a beautiful bouquet of gardenias and white roses. The girls carried hideous blooms that had this giant green thing sticking out of them (I have no idea how we ended up with those flowers). I hated those flowers, but again, didn't stress and didn't much care—this day was not about flowers.

The limousine drove down streets lined with thousands of Buffalonians, all out to give us their best wishes. I felt like the hometown girl coming home to people who loved me.

I stepped out of the car, eager to marry the man I was (and still am) so in love with.

Kirk

At the church, we had our own challenges. It was sweltering and muggy, like moist towels on a radiator. We had packed our guests as tight as humanly possible.

Another issue to contend with was security. Chelsea's brother had made a sweep of the chapel before the ceremony. He found photographers hiding in the confessionals in the back of the church. Our minister then took him aside and told him that a priest was sitting in the second row, but that his collar wasn't right.

Chelsea's brother approached the man in the collar. "Hi. How are you doing?" he asked. "Are you a friend of the bride or the groom?"

"I'm a good friend of the bride's father. We went to Holy Cross University in Boston together," said the man in the pew.

Knowing that his father never went to college, Chelsea's brother realized this was not a priest, but an imposter. "No, you didn't," he retorted. "Get out."

The man was removed.

Moments before the wedding, I asked my groomsmen to pray with me. I began to pray from a place of such gratitude for Chelsea that I cried. "Lord, thank You. You've been so *kind* to me. Next to the day I found You, this is the most wonderful day of my life. I promise that I will love this woman 'til I die."

I'm sure Chelsea's brother was a bit weirded out by the shameless emotion. After all, this was his *sister*. But my prayer was no more strange than having to kick a fake priest out of church!

We stood, and I was ready to meet my bride.

We stepped into the sanctuary, now matching the temperature of the equator. I waited as my beautiful sisters walked down the aisle. That was nice, but there was only one person I wanted to see.

Then she appeared in the doorway, backlit by the blazing sun.

She was absolutely, stunningly beautiful—ravishingly gorgeous. Time seemed to stand still, then crept to slow motion as she approached me.

Her mom escorted her down the aisle. She wore a white wedding dress beautifully fitted to her perfect form. I could not believe that I was the man who got to marry this beautiful girl. As she came toward me, I was overwhelmed by the goodness of God to give me this angel in white. Silently, I resolved in my heart to always honor, protect and cherish her.

Chelsea

The people of Buffalo were wonderful. After the ceremony, they chased us all over town, so it was challenging to move around, but they didn't ruin a thing.

At the reception, held at a small country club, my brother gave a special toast, talking a lot about my dad. I missed my father a lot, but was so grateful that he had met Kirk. That took a little of the sting out of his absence.

Our reception was *so fun*. The guests danced and laughed and there was such joy. Everyone had a great time. I cannot think of any way the day could have been better (well, except the flowers!).

After the reception, we slipped away to our special spot, the Asa Ransom Inn, where we spent our wedding night. Our honeymoon was short and sweet—two days mountain biking in Vermont—because we were due back to work.

Kirk

Chelsea and I returned to the set with apprehension for the start of the final season (season 7), united in holy matrimony. Not only had I not invited my cast members or producers to the wedding, but due to our strained relationships, I had neglected to even inform them of our upcoming nuptials. Because it was the middle of summer and the show was on hiatus, they found out by watching the news. (Gulp.)

In my immaturity, I made a poor choice that created even more tension and a lot of hurt feelings. But hindsight is always 20/20.

If I had it to do over again, I would tell the cast we were engaged. Happy for me or not, I should have told them.

Chelsea also wished I had talked to the cast. It may not have changed any hurt feelings, but at least they would have understood why we were having a small, private wedding. Regardless, it would have been a better way to handle it.

The Wedding Sermon

Once upon a time, far away—but not too long ago—a young woman met a young man, and not her knight in shining armor, but someone even better: He was just what she was looking for. The right qualities were there: honesty, integrity, affection, humor, faith and openness. He was a man in the Lord, living life with an open mind, open hands, open heart. So it seemed perfectly natural for her to fall in love with him, to want to share her life with him forever.

And the guy was just as thrilled with what he discovered in this sensitive and alert young woman. She was interested and interesting—a real class act. She captured his imagination; he couldn't get her off his mind! Her personality was intriguing, her family delightful, her deep faith very evident. He had no choice but to fall hopelessly in love with her.

And so one day they got married. Today, in fact.

The funny part about this story is that it is not a fairy tale; it is not a made-for-TV movie; no, it's a true story. A love story. A story that we see unfolding right before our very eyes.

Chelsea met Kirk, and Kirk met Chelsea, and now nothing will ever be the same again. The Lord has gently and wonderfully, even playfully, brought you together, and a new promise has been born: the promise of love, of life together, of the two of you facing God and the future hand in hand.

Over a period of time, Chelsea and Kirk, you've come to realize that love takes a lot of work. It takes time. It takes effort. But most of all, it takes God to help you create it afresh again and again in the face of heartache and heartbreak. It takes God to help you appreciate and enjoy and enrich your love for each other.

In spite of everything, Chelsea and Kirk, love is worth it. Love is worth every ounce of energy we give. And we know the two of you can do it: You both have the strength of faith and family to support you, and so we are confident. We have all felt your love for us, and we have all seen your love for each other grow ever so slowly, ever so surely, ever so deeply.

I can't say that you "lived happily ever after" . . . only you can tell us that part of the story. It will take the rest of your life to finish out the story. But if the "pilot" is any indication, you're off to a great start—and along the way, we'll all be your most loyal and devoted fans.

We gather today to celebrate your promises, and to pray that the story of your love will continue on and on—deepening, developing, mellowing. And it will, Chelsea and Kirk, if you keep working at the script of your love and marriage. Keep working at it with the Lord. Keep working at it with each other. Keep working at it with love.

The secret, Chelsea and Kirk, is that you keep falling in love with each other day after day for the rest of your lives.

Rev. Ronald Mierzwa
July 20, 1991

Chapter 18

The Honeymooners

As young marrieds, we quickly discovered that our personalities are as different as chalk and cheese.

I tend to talk about things in an overly polite, politically correct manner. To Chelsea, this means beating around the bush. She likes to hit things head on. "Say what you mean! Don't mask it with all this other stuff! Shoot straight."

At restaurants, I tip a precise amount. Chelsea likes to over-tip. Early in our relationship, she'd slip the waiter a $20 bill on our way out—*after* I'd already tipped him! I was thinking about college funds and she was saying, "Did you ever wait tables? They deserve it."

If we get chips and salsa, I ask for the mild, sweeter salsa. Chelsea orders the wrath-of-God salsa. She says, "Give me garlic sardines and oysters!" while I say, "Show me the vanilla pudding."

Chelsea is very passionate, so when she communicated her strong, fierce opinions about something, I used to think she was mad at me. She wasn't. She's just an Italian who expresses her opinions more strongly than I was used to.

Married life quickly brought out other differences between us. One day we were cleaning up after dinner. We had used our best china and Chelsea was rinsing a crystal goblet in the sink. She accidentally dropped it, breaking it into tiny, pricey pieces of glass.

I (Mister Economical) couldn't believe it. *"Honey!* You have to be careful with those. They're expensive."

Chelsea

I was shocked. I could not believe he had just scolded me for a *mistake*.

I have no idea what came over me, but I grabbed another crystal glass, looked Kirk right in the eye—and dropped it. It shattered in the cast iron sink.

He stood there and didn't say a word, but I could see it on his face: *I married a psychopath.*

Growing up in my home, it was never about loving stuff. If you dropped something, nobody worried about it. My dad was fixing a piano leg one day and hadn't removed all of my mother's glass heirlooms. The piano collapsed. None of the crystal survived. My mom brushed it off, saying, "Ah, those antiques made me have to dust too much anyway."

I knew my mom's heart was breaking. The items had strong sentimental value. But she would never have made my dad feel bad about his butter fingers. She knew it was a mistake.

Kirk

We laugh about it now. These days if Chelsea breaks something, I've learned to say, "Hey, it's just a thing. Break another one!"

We moved into a condo on the lake in Calabasas, California. During the day, we hiked the Santa Monica Mountains with our dogs, Micah, a monstrous Rhodesian ridgeback, and Rosie, a mutt of unknown heritage.

We hiked to the top to enjoy the sunset, able to see seven other peaks from our lookout. Sometimes we'd return home and make gourmet meals. We both love to cook. Only once did a culinary experiment fail (couscous pizza—never again).

Chelsea

Five years into our marriage, we took a second honeymoon to Italy. One backpack, three weeks, no reservations. It was the most amazing trip—romantic and spontaneous (which freaked my structured husband a bit).

It was everything I could dream of in a honeymoon. We stopped at a train station and said, "We're looking for a place to stay." The people were more than helpful and we always ended up in some charming villa or tiny romantic hotel room.

Rome. Milan. Florence. One time we found ourselves staying in the rooftop suite of an elegant hotel, overlooking all of Venice, paying next to nothing at all.

We hiked up the hillsides of Italy and had lunch in hidden farmhouses, eating bruschetta and fish cooked on an open fire. Our favorite honeymoon pastime was stopping in the middle of fragrant olive orchards to enjoy the afternoon in private.

The trip was very romantic, loaded with incredible memories. We laughed a lot, so in love. It was, without a doubt, the best trip of my life.

Kirk

Once *Growing Pains* ended, we had some free time on our hands. Now sitcom-less, I found myself with time to pursue some of the quirky interests I had never been able to chase during the time-consuming years spent growing up on television. As a result, Chelsea moans whenever someone mentions the word "hobby."

I'm not a multi-tasker. I pour my entire focus into one thing at a time, which means that every time I had a hobby in those early years, I went overboard. Take Micah, for example. I took him to every dog training class possible. I bought books on dog training. We worked for months. I spent hours and hours every day training him to be a protection dog for Chelsea and the kids. I learned so much, I could've opened a dog psycho-therapy business myself.

One of my more odd (but productive) hobbies was becoming a horticulturist. I spent hours memorizing different types of roses and planting them in our yard. I took branches of trees and vines, intertwining them to make arbors and railings. I worked long hours fashioning beautiful gardens in our backyard.

On the environmental front, when I discovered how many gallons of water were wasted through our water filtration system, I decided to create a gray water system and use that water to irrigate the garden. I had a compost pile and started recycling as much of our trash as possible.

Being a gadget lover, I had a solar oven that, if you pointed it at the right spot in the sky, would heat up to 350 degrees. On hot summer days, I made many a delicious meal in that baby, dishes that would make Mario Batali proud.

Given that my time had freed up, my Grandpa Frank taught me how to golf. We spent many mornings hitting the links together. He gave me a book called *The Modern Fundamentals of Golf—Five Lessons* by Ben Hogan. I studied the book and liked Hogan so much that I bought a set of Hogan Edge clubs. These are forged iron rather than the cast-molded clubs that most people use today. They're harder to hit—but Ben Hogan used them, so I would too.

Chelsea and I threw a lot of theme parties when we were first married. *Passion, Pasta and Pistols* was one of them. Our guests arrived in costume and in character and remained in character all night. We threw '60s and '70s bashes—even '80s-themed nights. (Though Chelsea would never have dreamed of wearing an "I HEART MIKE SEAVER" shirt back in the day, she proudly wears one now. Apparently, I'm "retro-chic," which is a feisty name for "old school.")

But the leisurely lifestyle we were living was about to change. A new party was about to start—one that began with a phone call.

Chapter 19

Family Ties

"Daddy, it stinks in here."

"Be there in a minute."

"Mommy says it's because there's dead rats under the house."

"Mommy might be right, Bella."

"Daddy . . ."

"Yes, Olivia?"

"Bella takes her chicken on the trampoline and makes it lay on her back and then she goes off and leaves the chicken on the trampoline and the chicken just lays on its back."

"Dad?"

"What's up, James?"

"Where's Whitie, Dad?"

"Whitie got too pecky," Olivia says, "so we sent her back."

"Daddy," Ahna says, snuggling close. "Can we roast the chestnuts yet?"

"Later, after Grandma and Grandpa come."

"When are we going fishing?"

"In a few minutes, Luke."

"Are you going to chaperone our space camp trip?"

"Jack, you know I wouldn't miss it for the world."

Daily conversation with my wife and kids . . . this is what I want forever. I have no control over time, but if I could keep my little troop just as they are, I'd be deeply tempted.

Chelsea and I have six—yes, *six*—kids. Saying that to folks always causes a physical reaction—a bodily response to the news. Many cover their mouths in shock, as if they're keeping their lunch down. *SIX?*

Yep . . . a nice, clean, even half-dozen.

Each of these kids was placed in our lives for a specific reason. Chelsea and I believe God masterminded every detail of our family.

Baby Calls

Five years into our marriage Chelsea looked at me and said, "Kirk, I think it's time we started thinking about a family."

I nodded. "That sounds about right."

"I'd like to adopt the first two," she said. "I want to build a family in this incredibly special way." Chelsea has a huge heart for adoption—she was adopted into a family where she was cherished and treasured. Her parents lavished love on her and she wanted to have the privilege of passing that along. "I want the first two to be adopted so they know they were our first choice."

"I'm in. Let's do it," I said. It's no small satisfaction when I'm able to help my wife's dreams come true. Besides, I wanted children and thought that adoption was an exciting option.

Not too long after that discussion, we met with an adoption agency and talked to a social worker.

When she asked what kind of child we wanted, we replied, "We're open to whatever baby God brings to us." She was surprised. Most families have very specific things they look for—we didn't. We wanted to love a child. To be a family. We told the social worker we'd take a hard-to-place baby.

"Even a bi-racial child?" she asked.

"Of course," we both answered in unison, surprised she even had to ask.

It wasn't long after we finished the adoption process that we got our first "baby call."

The social worker called, jazzed: "I think I might have someone for you. How soon could you be ready?"

"Today," Chelsea told her.

She laughed. "We don't need you today, but very, very soon. In a week, even."

That day, we went out and bought a crib, a car seat, bottles and diapers. When the call came, we flew to a town and waited for the social worker to bring us an incredible boy we named Jack. We stayed one night and returned to our condo in Calabasas, now with a precious gift of God in our hands who was already embedded in our hearts.

A year later, the social worker called again. Isabella joined our family just as our new home was being remodeled.

Nine months later: another call, another girl. Ahna arrived just as we moved into our home, almost as if she'd known we had space to fill.

A year later Luke was welcomed into our family.

So much for adopting two! But Chelsea and I knew that each of these kids was meant to be *ours*.

Plumbing Issues

When Luke was a few months old, Chelsea leaned against the changing table, wiping clean another baby bottom and said, "Hon, would you go check the bathroom for me? Something's up with the sink."

Feeling like Bob Vila or Ty Pennington, I crawled my manly self under the sink for a quick look-see. The faucet worked fine. No visible leaks in the pipes. Except for a couple of long strands of hair in the sink (which Chelsea always leaves behind as a gift for me), there was nothing clogging the drain.

But what was this? A little white stick that looked like it belonged in a packet of Fun Dip. *Wait, what's this plus-sign? Weird.*

The dim light slowly grew brighter. Then the bulb went on. I raced from the bathroom. "You're pregnant!"

Chelsea smiled and nodded, and—in congratulation—tossed me Ahna's dirty diaper to take to the trash.

When Olivia appeared, I flew out of the delivery room and threw myself on Mom. I sobbed like a little girl on Christmas morning who'd gotten the Baby Alive Doll she'd always dreamed of.

In keeping with Cameron tradition, my entire family was present in the waiting room. We all attend the births of every baby born into the family. This time, it was my turn to be the father coming out to announce to the world, "It's a girl!"

A few months later, I arrived home and Chelsea said, "Hey, toss me a clean binky, would ya?" (Not the greeting a celebrity expects, but I was certainly getting used to it.)

I brought her a pacifier, just as the kids tackled me from four corners of the room. Chelsea plugged the baby's crying and turned to me, "Kirk, there's another problem with the bathroom sink."

Nine months later, James became the new baby of the family.

The Team

I can't imagine any of my kids not being here. Each is special. Each brings something unique to our family.

Jack

Lego genius. Loves B-ball. Gentle giant. By the time he's 15, I picture myself reprimanding him by saying, "Son, sit down and look me in the eye when I talk to you." Jack recently discovered Ford Mustangs, good music and girls. (That's my boy!)

Isabella

Everything about her is larger than life: personality, smile and wild curly hair. Bella knows how to have a good time. Her energy level can go from 0 to 60 in 3 seconds flat. She shares a room with her sister Ahna and I know they're going to be best friends for life.

Ahna

Her biggest dream is to be a good mom. Ahna has a natural compassion and tenderness that would've inspired Mother Teresa. And she's such a *girl*—hats, gloves, heels, creams, nail polish and perfumes. She's 8 going on 28!

Luke

Frog-catching enthusiast, fisherman and natural comedian. So sweet and cuddly—the boy next door. Luke looks up to his big brother Jack and loves to drive him crazy any chance he gets.

Olivia

Olivia looks like Chelsea in miniature. She has me wrapped—I'm reduced to a puddle when I think of her in a white wedding dress. For now, she is content with the idea of marrying her daddy. She loves gardens, fairy houses, nature and animals. She is strong and opinionated (like someone else I know).

James

He's Daddy's Little Helper. Whatever I'm doing, he's game to do it with me. He always uses the name "Dad" when he talks to me. "I'm helping, aren't I, Dad? We're the guys, right, Dad? Hey, Dad . . . can I help you bring in the firewood, Dad?" He's absolutely in love with my wife. If he catches me kissing her, it's a full body tackle to recover his possession.

At Home

Kirk

We live in a ranch style home surrounded by mountains. It's built durable so that the kids can be kids—running around, down the hall, through the kitchen, living room and back. Our walls are decorated with photos of the kids and children's artwork.

The backyard is our favorite room of the house. We planted a trampoline in the ground, just like my grandparents did. We have a creek running behind the house where we go fishing, a campfire pit to roast marshmallows and a tire-swing under an enormous California oak tree. I built a chicken coop so the kids can harvest eggs. My office is in a small, refurbished tool shed on a spit of land sticking into the creek. I go out there to get away from the perpetual noise when I need to, but am still close enough for anything interesting that pops up throughout the day.

Our house is a home—a haven of safety and family. There's almost always laundry on the kitchen table, or crafts, paper and paints. There are kids constantly calling, talking, shrieking, playing. There's Chelsea acting out some silly skit or leading the kids in an interpretive dance.

She's the most amazing mother. When I have to travel—yet again—the kids groan, "Oh, Daddy. Do you *have* to go?"

"Who would you rather go away, me or Mommy?"

"*You!*" the unhesitant chorus of voices shouts.

During the down time of raising six children (yeah, right), Chelsea somehow finds the energy to teach and mentor a group of mothers in a parenting class at our kids' school.

Chelsea

It may seem like I've got a lot on my plate, but life is great. It's kept exciting in part by a husband who grew up as a comedy actor.

To this day, Kirk makes me laugh like no one else. He falls down the stairs and I laugh. (When anyone else falls down stairs, I call the paramedics.) I first saw it years ago when we attended a black-tie affair. He tripped *up* the stairs, then tripped *down* the stairs—on purpose. He looked around and said loudly, "Man, somebody's gotta fix that stair—it could really hurt someone." I lost it in the audience, laughing at my goofball husband.

Another time we were at a televised celebrity ski event. Everyone was trying to show off. Right before Kirk's turn to go up the lift, he said, "Chelsea, watch this."

Halfway down the run he started flailing his poles.

The announcer remarked, "Oh! Cameron looks like he's having a little trouble. Uh, uh, uh, *ohhhhhhh!*"

Kirk crossed his poles and intentionally did a major fall, landing on his face, right in front of the camera.

"Oh! A bad day for Kirk!" the announcer cried out.

I started laughing uncontrollably. Someone turned to me and said, "Chelsea, you need to go see if he's okay."

I said, "He's not okay. He's insane."

His brand of insanity keeps our home life fun. I wouldn't have it any other way.

Not All About Me

Kirk

If you've been to the website for the Way of the Master ministries or if you've seen me interviewed on television, maybe it seems as if I have life all figured out.

I hate to give false impressions.

I've been the center of attention my whole life. Whenever I walk into a room, whispers start bouncing off the walls.

"Look! There's Kirk Cameron!"

"Is that Mike Seaver?"

Strangers care about what I think. People are interested in what I have to say. People always laugh at my jokes . . . even when they aren't funny.

Since I was nine years old, people have been singing my praises. I've gotten such a steady diet of approval that my gut, to some extent, expects it. Part of me sees admiration as the norm. And somewhere in my subconscious, I depend too much on that kind of validation.

I hate admitting that. It makes me a little sick, just putting the words to paper.

A kid raised on a farm thinks nothing of chopping heads off chickens, while the rest of the world cringes at the thought. A child who spends his entire life preparing for the Olympics thinks it's normal to spend all day, every day, intensely training. When approval is all you know, your sense of reality is tweaked—though you don't see it because, to you, it's "normal."

In my early life's journey, I grew accustomed to being universally loved. It has been a struggle to die to self and to do the right thing without having an audience applaud me. I now know that I don't deserve that false sense of importance, but it took awhile.

Chelsea

There's no doubt about it: Kirk is used to a lot of validation and a lot of applause. Kirk often attached himself to places that validated him a lot, because that is what has fed him his whole life. Because of the abnormal adoration, it was challenging for him to understand what life was really about, who he really was and whose applause he was really trying to get.

In real life, there's not a lot of that kind of treatment. For actors used to applauding fans, it can be hard walking into a room where you're not always the center of attention. I'm glad when Kirk gets home from a trip, but the kids and I aren't going to flick on lighters and start swaying.

Tunnel Vision

Kirk

Another thing I struggle with is having tunnel vision—becoming too myopic. When I find something I'm excited about or interested in, I drop everything else and pour all my time, thoughts and energy into it.

I focus so hard and throw my whole heart into whatever it is so much that everything else in my life can suffer. This intense focus can be a good thing for a reasonable time, but when left unchecked is tough on anything and everyone who is not in the center of that focus.

When I was a kid, it was nature, lizards and snakes. Then for a while, it was the Rubik's Cube and Atari games. Later came acting, golf, gourmet cooking and a host of other activities. Each thing I took an interest in, I had to master.

They might be positive things such as working out at the gym, investing in a charitable cause like Camp Firefly or spending time with a friend who needed my help. I certainly turned this focus on Chelsea, the night she sat on my parents' fireplace and told me she felt the same way I did. There was no turning back. I gave all of my heart, soul, time and energy to our relationship—to the exclusion of everyone else.

Sometimes when I throw myself into something so wholeheartedly, other things in my life wither and dry up by simple neglect. When it's people who are neglected, wounded or abandoned in the process, then it becomes a serious issue.

When I turned to the Lord, knowing God became my passion. There is nothing wrong with having a desire to deeply know God and to serve Him—that's one of the places where my laser beam focus has served me very well. But even a love for ministry can become dangerous for me if I don't keep it in perspective. Ministry is notorious for feeding egos and destroying families. In my efforts to "reach the world," I have learned to be very careful that I don't neglect my own family.

Chelsea

Early in our relationship, it surprised Kirk when I didn't agree with him about this or that. He's often surrounded by "yes-men"—everyone saying yes to whatever he asks for. But with me, he always gets an honest response.

It wasn't that Kirk was intentionally selfish; he was just conditioned by a world that revolved around him. Home life is far more challenging than being a star on the road, and it requires much more giving rather than getting. It involves continually thinking of others before yourself. The addition of each child in our house has caused us both to become more and more selfless.

We've been married for 17 years now. Our house is a real home, with real people and real life challenges. If Kirk gets praise from the kids or me, it has nothing to do with his image and I know that means so much more to him than empty applause.

Conflict with Conflict

Kirk

I don't like conflict. When I need to confront someone about something, I often don't. That may sound like an inconsistency with the circumstances on the set of *Growing Pains*, but it isn't: My dislike of conflict is the reason it was agony to confront those men whose opinions and position I'd always respected.

I really want people to like me. Naturally, I'm a people pleaser. I've made my living off of being likable. That's that card that a celebrity plays—his likeability. It's easy for me to fall into the trap of being a people pleaser.

You might ask, "What's wrong with pleasing people?" Nothing. But when you avoid conflict at all costs, you let other people direct your life instead of standing on your own convictions.

Chelsea

We have the same issues all marriages have. *All* marriages take work. If you really want something good with your husband, you have to work *hard* at it.

In ours, we have the additional circumstance of living a *big* life. Kirk has a big career and ministry, with lots of travel. I have a big job as a mom. It's incredibly challenging having so many little kids and trying to keep the two of us connected. But I'm a pretty independent, strong girl. When he travels, I make the ship go. When he steps back onto this ship, it's an adjustment for all of us. *Okay, so now you're the Captain?*

God brought two people together with very different personalities, but we are so good for each other.

We have to forgive. We have to be able to believe in a better day—to persevere and understand commitment. We're continually working hard on all those things. I know that Kirk will never give up on this marriage and he knows I won't, either.

God is shepherding us and getting us through. Every time we get to a new pasture, I think, *I'm so glad we stuck that hard season out.* We have grown so much in 17 years. God just refines us somehow.

Chapter 20

Camp Firefly

Every week at the end of tape night, fans with special passes lined up to greet the cast backstage. Most special to me were kids in wheelchairs or on crutches or who had some kind of tubing device that helped them breathe. These kids had the most astounding wish—to meet Mike Seaver—before they died. These critically or terminally ill children had their dreams carried out through the Make-A-Wish Foundation or the Starlight Foundation.

My heart was touched by these kids, who asked for so little. I spent as much time as I could with them. Sometimes my mother invited them to her house for an after-tape party, or we took them out to dinner. Mom and Dad bought giant white teddy bears as mementoes to take home. Occasionally, if the children were too sick to travel, I'd try to call them.

Mom and associate producer Joey Scott put their heads together and found other ways to highlight these children and make them feel special. The announcer might introduce them—by name—as a special guest. The spotlight slid across the audience to highlight a beaming face. "I have something special for Billy," I said, as I walked to the Seaver closet and pulled out a *Growing Pains* jacket with his name embroidered on it.

Although it took six to eight months to have those wishes fulfilled, once the date came closer to arriving on the set of *Growing Pains*, the child often started showing signs of recovery. It was a strange phenomenon. It seemed as if the kids were determined to let nothing get in the way of their dream coming true.

Once they arrived at the studio, often by way of a limousine ride, they perked up even more. One girl had a difficult time breathing and was on a respirator and a feeding tube. Her mom began crying as she shared with us, "This is the first time in 10 years that Melissa has said, 'Mommy, I'm hungry.'" That little girl was so enthralled that for a brief moment, everything worked and she forgot about her disease.

We were all very aware that after these wishes were fulfilled, many children deteriorated pretty quickly because either there was nothing more for them to look forward to, or because their disease simply took over. Consequently, it was hard for Mom, Joey and me to let the night end. It was incredibly hard to say goodbye. We knew we would never see these kids again.

I can't take much credit for these events. I just showed up and loved the kids. Mom did most of the work and had the most creative ideas for making the fulfillment of their wishes very special. Joey helped run interference and get things completed.

Once we connected so much with a family that Joey and Mom arranged something very special for Christmas. They had a limo sent to pick up the family at the airport. The driver, dressed as Santa, held a sign with the little girl's name on it in the middle of the airport where everyone could see how important she was.

Joey and Mom bought a huge, life-sized stuffed animal and tucked it in the limo's back seat with a note from me saying that I couldn't wait to meet her and her family.

They came to the show and had a great time. As an added surprise, Joey and Mom arranged to have the cast waiting for them with a cake at a really fun restaurant. When we arrived, everything was set up like a big party. Because or our high recognition factor, everyone in the restaurant wondered who the cast of *Growing Pains* was waiting for. *It must be someone very special.* The joy on the family's faces was something we never forgot.

We said goodbye, which was very hard for the little girl. What she didn't know was that the party wasn't over yet.

The next morning, Joey and I were waiting for her in the lobby of the hotel. She thought we had simply come to say another goodbye and was very sad—until we swept her off to Disneyland for the day.

Once, a boy named Brandon came to the show through the Starlight Foundation. He suffered from a severe heart condition. It was his dream to have a family like Ben Seaver, my character's younger brother. His parents were divorced, and he felt like the Seavers were the perfect family. He spent the day with Jeremy Miller. I remember signing a photo for him, writing "God bless you" above my autograph.

Years later, while on the set of the first *Left Behind* film, I received a letter and newspaper clipping from Brandon. The article spoke of Brandon's miraculous recovery and how—even more impressively—he was at the top of his class at Louisiana Tech University and would be starting medical school at Tulane the following fall. His dream was to work side by side with the doctor who had saved his life.

I just had to talk to him personally, so we connected by phone. Brandon told me that the autograph I'd signed all those years ago had encouraged him throughout his medical ups and downs. He felt that God really did love him and had plans for his future.

Brandon not only reconnected with Jeremy during the filming of the *Growing Pains* reunion movie in New Orleans, he also found out that he would be working with his own doctors at Texas Children's Hospital after his graduation. Brandon is now in his fellowship at the Mayo Clinic, on his way to becoming a pediatric cardiologist—a heart doctor for seriously ill children. He often stays at our home when he's visiting California. Jeremy even comes over once in a while and cooks for him and our family.

The Spark of an Idea

Over the years, it was hard not to notice some very important dynamics in these families—namely, the huge weight on the shoulders of the parents. Their lives literally stopped when a seriously ill child came into their lives. Every minute and every dollar were spent on the medical needs to sustain their child's life. They no longer had any time or money to spend with their spouse or with the other children in the family. All attention was focused on the sick child.

About the time I met Chelsea, I felt something more needed to be done for these exhausted, strapped, stressed families. The idea came up to have a special summer camp for them. Mom put her amazing creativity to work. I told her some of what I envisioned, but left most of the brain and legwork up to her. I trusted her, and knew she would come up with great ideas.

Mom began searching for a venue for the camp and, through a friend, discovered a resort outside of Pine Mountain, Georgia, called Callaway Gardens. Callaway has 13,000 acres of land, including a 3,000-acre wilderness preserve, fishing, lakes, bicycle and hiking trails, 36 holes of golf, an Azalea garden and the world's largest manmade, white-sand beach on a lake.

The more Mom researched, the more she knew this would be the perfect place. With help from good friends Mark Collins and Lisa West, the first Camp Callaway began to take shape. The first retreat in 1989 set the stage for what the camp would look like, stand for and give to the families of seriously ill children.

Mom has since handed over the job of organizing the camp to Chelsea. The camp has changed names from Camp Callaway to Camp Firefly, but much of what Mom began still happens each year at this magical place.

Some friends of ours in Buffalo helped us come up with the new name. We loved it for two reasons—fireflies are light, and hope is light. We want to bring the light of hope to these families—that they can always be a family, no matter what happens. We also loved it because Camp Firefly is *filled* with fireflies. They are everywhere at nighttime. The kids catch them in jars and watch them light up like fairies.

How the Magic Happens

The process begins when Chelsea and I contact pediatric doctors and social workers throughout the nation. They send us a list of their three highest recommendations of children whom they feel would most benefit from the experience, and who are medically able to travel to Georgia. The whole family situation is considered, and we try to "gift" the families who don't have the resources to do something like Camp Firefly on their own.

Once Chelsea and I have the recommendations, we choose the families through much prayer and discussion. We try to blend and match families in some meaningful ways. For example, we try to get two single-mom families at camp the same week so that they likely have one person who understands their situation. We try to match the ages of the children so that everyone has someone to hang out with.

Most retreats for seriously ill children are for the child himself—a camp for kids with cancer, or kids with diabetes or cystic fibrosis. They usually go solo, without their siblings or parents. Camp Firefly, however, runs on a unique principle: We recognize that the entire family is affected by a child's illness. We understand that well children are often left behind, with all the attention focused on their sick sibling. The parents rarely see each other—and when they do, it's very stressful because they must always be focused on the sick child. By bringing *entire families* to camp, we hope we can generate togetherness, family wholeness, bonding and healing.

Camp Firefly is designed to bring laughter back into the lives of stressed-out families. For husbands to see their wives as the sweetheart they married. For wives to fall in love with their husbands again. For kids from all the families, sick and well, to connect with each other quickly, because these are people who understand exactly what their lives are like.

The families never know they are being considered for the camp— we don't want to hurt feelings or cause disappointment if they are not chosen. The first time they hear about it is when they receive a phone call from one of our staff members with an invitation to attend. Once they accept, Chelsea and I call and let them know we are excited to meet them. The families don't have to do anything but pack their clothes and wait for their itinerary. From that point on, everything is taken care of for them.

A car often picks the family up from their home and takes them to the airport, where they board a plane to Georgia. All the families arrive about the same time—thanks to Smokin' Jo Bullard, our friend at Delta Airlines who donates her time to work out the details for us.

The families arrive at camp to find luxury cars for their use while they are at the resort. Bill and Barbara Florence, owners of a Lexus dealership in the area, are incredibly generous to lend us these vehicles.

The staff helps to load the cars and then leads each family to the three- or four-bedroom villa they will call home for the next week. Nestled on forested hillsides, each place has a fully equipped kitchen, a washer and dryer, a large living area, a sundeck, a patio and a screened porch. We stock each villa with the family's favorite breakfast foods, muffins, cookies, snacks and fruits. In the fridge, there's bacon, eggs, orange juice and milk. Each bedroom has a pair of new sneakers for each family member, toys, T-shirts, pants, shorts and stuffed animals for the little ones. The parents find books, chocolates and other goodies on their beds.

Once settled, everyone gathers at the pool for a fiesta welcome buffet, where we all get to know each other a little.

The first year, I was unsure how to set the mood for the camp, so I picked up my sister Bridgette and threw her into the pool with all her clothes on. Within minutes, many of the staff members and guests were also in the pool, dressed head to toe in clothes plastered to their skin. They didn't need much more of a hint. From that point on, all masks fell away, and the happiness of simply living bubbled over. Since then, I've learned less drastic ways of getting people to connect. I've also learned that people in such tough situations connect with each other on their own very quickly. They don't need a lot of coaxing. They, of all people, understand the preciousness of time.

After our welcome dinner, the families hear about the following day's activities.

Each day is a different theme. One day we go to the beach and have a luau. The kids—sick and well—ride boogie boards, water skis and innertubes. Some even take the jet skis out for a spin.

One day we have a barbecue, topped off with a barn dance.

On Circus Day, we go to the big top where circus performers train. The children get to try out the trapezes and trampolines. I sometimes teach magic tricks.

There are sing-a-longs, s'mores and bike rides for those who are able.

One very special day, the dads all play golf together, the kids have a very special day of their own and the moms get a makeover. Sometimes a husband tears up when he sees his sweetheart looking just like the woman he fell in love with. That evening, the couples go to the restaurant on the grounds and share a candlelit dinner. For most, it's the first time in months or years they have been able to connect and be romantic.

People wonder how the kids can do all these things when they are so incredibly sick. What Chelsea and I have learned about sick children is that their spirits can be unbelievably strong. They may have medical tubes coming out of various limbs, but they just tape 'em down and join in the fun! *They're kids*. And they're living.

Chelsea says, "Camp shows you that as long as you're here, you're living, not dying. These kids don't live like they're dying . . . they live like they're living."

Camp helps them feel alive. It helps kids be kids. It helps the entire family to forget about the illness for a week. This gives them a chance to re-bond and heal as a family.

It doesn't take long to forget who is sick and who isn't. Everyone is so full of life. We learn so much from these families. They love in a way we have yet to learn. They understand that time is precious.

By the time the week is over, new, lifelong friendships have developed. These friendships are so strong that the families often return to camp reunions—often without the child who was the reason they had come in the first place.

Sacred Trust

After 18 years of Camp Firefly, we are still totally hands-on. Chelsea is the one who does most of the work organizing and overseeing. It's a huge task, but one she wouldn't give up for the world. We see this as a camp that God has entrusted to us, and we always want to be good stewards of His precious gifts.

Chelsea and I love going to camp. Our kids love it, too. Yes, we go as a family. We look forward every June to when we can make new friends. While we're there we are facilitators, but sometimes we are witnesses of miracles that take place before our eyes. Not miracles in the sense that the sick children suddenly are healed, but in the way families share a new light in their eyes. We see families connect with other families, bonding in ways that rarely happen in the rest of the world.

Chapter 21

The Narrow Road

If you disappear from the public consciousness for nine minutes, people wonder when you're going to make a "comeback." The weird thing is, you haven't really gone anywhere. Just because you're not reporting to work on a soundstage doesn't mean you've ceased to exist.

I still wake up every morning and put my parachute pants on one leg at a time. (Just seeing if you're still paying attention—the 'chutes have retired to the attic over the garage. The Smithsonian passed up my offer of a donation.)

A few years after *Growing Pains* said farewell to the American public, some folks came to me with a script called *Kirk* (which seemed perfect for me, considering the title). It was a sitcom for the WB network (now the CW) that ran for two years. I played a 20-something guy who had "inherited" his three younger siblings when their great-aunt couldn't care for them anymore. "Kirk" was an advertising guy low on the totem pole in New York City, living as a bachelor in a small apartment. Across the hall lived the beautiful yet untouchable doctor-in-training, Elizabeth—played by Chelsea. I wore a Band-Aid over my wedding ring because I didn't want to take it off—not even for a sitcom.

We attempted to make a sweet and heartwarming show, just as family sitcoms started going out of vogue in the mid-'90s. Boundary-pushing shows like *Friends* and *Seinfeld* were the new norm, while shows like *Cosby* and *Family Ties* were slipping away.

Where Was I Now?

It doesn't take long for channels like E! or shows like *ET* and *Extra* to start asking "Where are you now?" People love to see what stars of the past are up to.

I think they just really enjoy seeing how we age.

Jack had been born and Chelsea and I were enjoying that chapter of life, but I wasn't working on a show and I didn't have anything particular going on in the way of ministry. I became uneasy. I felt like my career gear-shifter had popped out of fourth and was sitting in neutral. I felt like I was wasting time, going nowhere. I found myself sitting in the living room, idly picking stray lint off my Members Only jacket. (Again, kidding.)

What should I do to make a living now? I asked myself. *Is my career over? Will I ever work on a sitcom again? Do I want to be in the biz, or should I go back to school like I've always planned?*

I dove into my hobbies to give myself something to do while I tried to sort through these big questions. I also began taking some seminary-level courses through Grace Community Church near our home. I enjoyed them so much, I thought I might like to get a degree in ministry.

God had other plans.

Left Behind

Chelsea shook me in the middle of the night.

"Kirk! Kirk! You've gotta read this book. It would make a *great* movie!"

She waved the book *Left Behind* in front of my barely opened eyes. I groaned, rolled over and tried to go back to sleep. But she was so excited that she wouldn't stop poking me. "Kirk, it would make such a great movie! I can just see you playing the part of Buck Williams, and I could play Hattie!"

"Yeah, yeah," I said and went back to sleep.

A few weeks later, my manager got a call from a guy who said, "We're doing this little film called *Left Behind*, and we wondered if Kirk would play the part of Buck Williams."

A reporter named Buck is one of those "left behind"
when the rapture removes all Christians from the Earth.

That was the plot of the book and film, a story that captured the imaginations of over 65 million readers of the novels in the series.

I read the script, but not the book. I liked it and agreed to play Buck. Then the producers asked Chelsea to play Hattie. She was so excited—her dream was coming true, and so shortly after she'd dreamed it. A few weeks later, we packed our family and moved to Toronto for six weeks of filming.

Each day before filming, I opened the book to read the scene we were slated to do that day, picking up the voice and actions of Buck Williams. I enjoyed working on the films, and I played Buck again for the second and third *Left Behind* movies.

What was ironic about the filming of the *Left Behind* movies is that there were very few Christians on the set. Chelsea and I, and possibly one other cast member, were the only believers. There was not even one open conversation on the set about God or Christ the whole time we shot the movie. Between takes and during lunch hours, I did my best to share my faith with as many cast and crew members as possible, but I still felt uneasy that most of the people had no understanding of who Christ is and what He has done. On the final day of shooting, I stood up in a cafeteria among the cast and crew and thanked them all for their hard work and great attitudes. Then I asked them to consider what *Left Behind* was all about—the return of Jesus Christ.

"What do you think will happen to you when you die?" I asked. Then I did my best to explain the gospel and urged each of them to turn their hearts to God. Despite my earnest plea, I got no applause from *that* audience.

One man, our Jewish photographer, walked up as I sat alone finishing my meal to let me know that he admired my courage to share my beliefs, even though he didn't agree with them. Later, when no one was watching, I heard from a couple of professing Christians who decided to "come out of the closet" to tell me that they loved the Lord but were to afraid to do so publicly for fear they would be shunned by the rest of the crew. The words of Jesus came to my mind: "For whoever is ashamed of Me and My words, of him the Son of Man will be ashamed when He comes in His own glory, and in His Father's, and of the holy angels" (Luke 9:26).

The Way of the Master

In the summer of 2000, I was at a booksellers convention to promote *Left Behind*, signing DVDs for the long line of people snaking through the aisles.

Some guy looked at me, handed me a CD and said, "You *have* to listen to this."

I tossed it on the pile of stuff I'd collected from the convention. Later, as I was driving to visit my grandmother, I popped the disc in and listened to the message. I thought it was interesting, but didn't quite get it. Six months later, someone sent me two copies of the same CD. I listened again as I was driving to a church to share my faith story with the congregation.

This time it grabbed me. *Now I get it. This is huge.*

The man's teaching was foundation shaking. It challenged so much of what I thought I knew about the gospel and how to share my faith with people in a way that is accurate and effective.

I called the phone number on the back of the CD and reached a ministry called Living Waters Publications. I asked to speak with Ray Comfort, the man preaching on the disc. I knew nothing about him, and I was surprised that I was able to reach him that easily. We started talking, and I asked if I could get more information on his ministry. He sent me the book called *God Has a Wonderful Plan for Your Life: The Myth of Modern Message*, which had a picture of Stephen the martyr being stoned on the cover.

Hmm, I thought. *That's an interesting way to talk about God's "wonderful plan" for Stephen's life—a guy getting bludgeoned by rocks. Cheery.*

I began to read, and it was like an atomic bomb went off inside me. This guy was saying things I'd been thinking about for so long but never heard anyone talk about. One hundred years ago people were all over this topic, yet I'd rarely heard any contemporary preachers talk the same way about the most important issue in history.

The book was all about sharing the gospel with people by addressing their moral conscience using the Law of God, rather than enticing them to "ask Jesus into their hearts" with the "God has a wonderful plan" hook. I considered what I read, knowing that no one had ever personally shared the gospel with me in that very specific manner. I thought, *I wonder what would happen if I witnessed to myself in this way?*

I got down on my knees and, like the book said, asked myself if I thought I was a good person. *Sure,* I thought. *Not perfect, but as good as anyone else. I've never murdered anyone.*

I then pulled out my Bible, opened it to Exodus 20 and went through the Ten Commandments, one by one, asking myself if I had broken them.

I certainly had failed to keep the first of the ten by not always loving God above all other things.

When I had made an "idol" by creating a god in my mind that I was comfortable with (see chapter 12), I had broken the second.

Taking God's name in vain, or using it disrespectfully, was just a part of my everyday speech as a kid. I used it to punctuate many a raunchy sentence.

Setting aside one day in seven to honor the God who had given me life seemed like a reasonable request, but had been the last thing on my mind for the first 17 years of my life.

Always honor my parents? Ha! *If they only knew* . . .

Murder? I thought I was safe with that one, but then I read Jesus' words about how God considers hatred to be murder and lust to be adultery—I was guilty on many counts of both.

I've stolen little stuff and big stuff—that made me a thief.

Greed? Being relatively wealthy, I had most of what I wanted, but I would be lying if I said I was fully content with what I had. I always had my eye on something more.

When I was done taking my moral inventory, it had a profound impact on me. For the first time, I *really* considered what it would be like to stand guilty before an all-powerful, all-knowing God, who could see my secret thought life and would judge right down to the thoughts and intentions of my heart. I became much more painfully aware of my own unworthiness. I came to grips with the fact that I was a self-admitted liar and a thief. According to Scripture, God also saw me as a murderer and an adulterer. In those heavy, soul-searching moments, I wanted to surrender my life to the Lord all over again—this time more completely.

Years earlier, I had grasped a basic understanding of the gospel and could articulate it, but after looking at myself through the lens of God's Law, I could now see a new depth to my sin. Now the book of Romans made sense when Paul said that through the commandments, his sin became "exceedingly sinful." In my early understanding of the gospel at 17 years old, I felt as though I had been forgiven of a relatively small infraction of the law—say, a $10 fine—and I was grateful. When I saw my sin in its *true* light (again, through the lens of the Commandments), I could see that the $10 fine was in reality a $10 million fine. I understood for the first time that the gospel is the good news that Jesus (Almighty God in human flesh) paid that fine for me on the cross with His life's blood, forgiving me for all my sins, freeing me from judgment and eternal punishment, rescuing me from Satan's power so I could become a dearly loved child of God, and granting me the incalculable riches and limitless joys that await me in heaven.

I was overwhelmed. This startling insight into my own heart gave me the ability to truly repent (which means to turn from sin and turn to God) on a deeper level, and it increased my love for the cross tenfold.

I wanted to share this new understanding with everyone I knew—and everyone I *didn't* know. Finally, I understood why trying to reconcile the existence of hell with a loving God is so hard for an angry atheist: They don't understand the depth of their sin. This approach explained it beautifully.

I watched a video of Ray open-air preaching in Central Park in New York City at a Hare Krishna convention. Everything he did was the opposite of what I had learned in church about evangelism. He stood on a little milk crate, making a spectacle of himself in the middle of a crowd. He wasn't preaching in a church, but pleading with people in a park. Some people were heckling him. Many others were listening attentively. He wasn't sporting trendy clothes and a freshly trimmed soul patch to connect with the crowd while he cracked jokes and told stories of how Jesus helped the poor. He was upfront about sin, Judgment Day, the cross, God's grace and eternity.

It was so cool. I felt like I was watching a modern-day Paul speaking to the people on Mars Hill, preaching to those who were worshiping their unknown god (see Acts 17:16-34). It was very inspiring.

Ray didn't badger or belittle his audience. He didn't yell. He reasoned with people and combined that with communicating God's Word in a way that made so much sense to his hearers. His approach was right in line with what I had read in the book he had given me. He wasn't a wild-eyed, crazy street-corner preacher wearing a sandwich board painted badly with the words *Turn or Burn!* or *Jesus is the Answer!*

This was more like a guy who had found the cure for cancer standing up saying, "Please, please, listen to what I'm telling you!" This man was telling the crowd, "I've found the cure to death, and you can have it—it's in Christ."

When I turned off the DVD, I called Ray again and said, "I'd like to have lunch with you."

I drove over an hour to his office, not knowing what to expect. Would he be a distinguished theological giant? No, he was a short but brilliant lunatic. He ran around his office like A.D.D. was on sale at Wal-Mart. He never walked—he trotted. At the restaurant, while the waitress led us to our table, he stopped at every other table along the way and handed out pamphlets called *101 of the World's Funniest One-liners*, which contained an editorial note explaining the way to find everlasting life. The guy was so bold. He seemed to have no fear talking to anyone. He was so out-there compared to what I had been exposed to regarding how to share my faith.

Honestly, I wanted to crawl under the table. *Oh no, he's one of those guys!* I thought. *Why couldn't I see this coming? How fast can I down my lunch and get out of here?*

We sat and talked for three hours. He was very sane and very real. I realized that I was very uncomfortable with his methods. When I looked around, I saw people reading the pamphlets. They weren't typical tracts—they were optical illusions or funny one-liners. I thought, *Wow, they aren't throwing them back at him. They aren't calling him names or giving him dirty looks.* People laughed reading them cover to cover. Some stopped by and thanked Ray, even asking him for more.

Funny pamphlets aside, I left still feeling uneasy about Ray's unconventional message. It was so counter-church-culture. I called people whose opinions I respected and asked, "Have you ever heard of Ray Comfort?"

Some said, "I have, and I really don't like him."

Others said they absolutely loved what he taught and it had changed their lives.

At first, getting involved with Ray seemed a little too controversial for me. I wanted to be the guy who makes everybody happy. I wanted everyone to like me. But no matter how many times I tried to shy away from it, I kept getting drawn back. His approach to sharing the gospel seemed too important. I became more and more convinced that it was something I wanted to be a part of.

Unexpected Expansion

Some time later, a large religious television network requested an interview with me on their flagship program. I agreed because I wanted to share my story of faith with a worldwide audience.

The day before I was supposed to appear, the producers called. The host had gotten sick and they wondered if I would host the two-hour program. I thought, *Sure . . . when pigs fly!* I had seen too many self-styled preachers on religious television making fools of themselves by running around in circles, falling over and begging for money to even consider being viewed as one of them.

I called Ray, the go-between for the interview. He said, "This is such a huge platform, and there are some very respected pastors on that network. You could speak the truth and get it to lots and lots of people who otherwise wouldn't hear what you have to say."

Together we agreed that if the Christian network would work with me and agree to my terms, I would do it. I needed to be comfortable with the guests coming in for interviews, and I wanted to preach the essence of Ray's message called "Hell's Best-Kept Secret."

TBN agreed. I went on the show, interviewed several people and preached a 45-minute sermon. To my surprise, the ratings were so high that the network asked me to host more programs.

I responded, "I don't think I would like to host, but what if Ray and I give you some half-hour videos that you can air as a series?"

They agreed and Ray and I created a show and curriculum out of the Living Waters ministry. We called it *The Way of the Master*. We began making videos that taught Christians how to share the gospel using the Ten Commandments—the way Jesus did (see Mark 10:17).

The shows were unique, but were well received by viewers. People especially enjoyed watching clips of street witnessing.

We continued making episodes and soon had 13 shows. The first year it won the National Religious Broadcaster's Best Program and People's Choice awards.

We've completed 39 episodes to date and are currently working on our fourth season. The show is broadcast on 20 networks in 70 countries and translated into several languages. We also started a radio program, hosted by Todd Friel. (Check it out at www.WayOfTheMasterRadio.com.)

No More Multi-tasking

Even though I loved my work on *The Way of the Master*, I was reluctant to tank my Hollywood career by getting too vocal about my faith. I didn't want to be known as "the religious guy."

But then I looked at the apostle Paul, who said (my paraphrase), "Am I trying to please God or to please man? If I'm trying to please man, what on earth am I doing being a Christian? Because I'm burning every bridge I've got. I've burned it with the Pharisees, I've burned it with all my contemporaries, I've burned everything and I consider all those things rubbish compared to the value of knowing Christ" (see Gal. 1:10; Phil. 3:8).

Jesus' words came to my mind, such as, "If any man will come after Me, let him deny himself, take up his cross daily and follow Me" (see Matt. 16:24).

"He who tries to save his life will lose it, he who loses his life for My sake will find it" (see Mark 8:35).

"He who does not forsake all he has cannot be My disciple" (see Matt. 10:38).

Why am I really holding back? I asked myself.

I was worried about pleasing people. I wanted to re-shift my focus onto pleasing the Lord, rather than pleasing Hollywood gatekeepers.

At the same time, I didn't want to lose the platform from which I had been able to speak about the Lord.

It was a big struggle. I didn't want to look like a fanatic, yet I could not deny being a believer in Jesus Christ—that's what defined me in the ultimate sense. Yet if people asked who I was or what was important to me, I would have to minimize or water down the answer in order to maintain my hip, celebrity image. On the other hand, I knew that the more I kept my faith secret, the less impact I could have on others.

My relationship with Kirk has come a long way—not that it was ever really bad. Mainly due to the age difference of six years, we just weren't really close.

The biggest factor in the change of our relationship is God. I was 12 when we started going to church. I said the sinner's prayer and asked Jesus to be the Savior of my life. From that point, I considered myself a Christian and opened my Bible every once in a while . . . once every few years.

About six years ago, there were some tough things going on in my life. I was searching and seeking. My brother sent me *The Way of the Master* book. Kirk didn't push me or bug me, but he called me like a loving brother and said, "Hey, Can . . . I want to send you this book and I hope you read it. It changed my life."

It sat on my shelf for a little while before I finally read it, at just the perfect time. God really revealed Himself to me. The first person I called was my brother. I remember being in tears saying, "Kirk, I get it. I understand." To hear the joy he had for me in his voice changed everything between us.

We talked about the past, about a couple of hurtful situations. We apologized for those things and started off on a new foot that day.

His faithfulness and willingness to care and love me and continue to care about my relationship with God—that's a difficult thing to do without turning people off or pushing them away. But it's had a huge ripple effect on my life.

I'm so appreciative that's the kind of man Kirk's grown into.

Candace Cameron, Kirk's sister

My balancing act between secular career and ministry was limiting. The more I pursued my acting career, trying to develop another TV series, the more time it consumed, and I lost focus on ministry. Attempting to find a middle ground between the two only meant that I rode both at half speed.

By the time I reached my 30s, I knew myself well enough to realize that the balancing act wouldn't work. I'm not a multi-tasker. I go full-throttle with whatever I spend my time doing. I asked myself, *Where is my heart? What am I passionate about? What can I totally throw myself into?*

That's when I prayed, "Lord, if good roles come up, I'll audition for them. I'll meet with producers, casting directors, whatever. But I don't want to fake who I am. I'm going full-steam with serving You. I need You to open and close the right doors."

Not everyone was thrilled with my new ministry ventures. I scheduled a meeting with my managers and took Ray along so they could get a feel for him. After all, we were working together on a highly visible show.

We talked some before I said, "Guys, be honest with me: Do you think I'm shooting myself in the foot by working with Ray and doing projects like *Left Behind* and *The Way of the Master*?"

"Yes," they said. "Your career is definitely going to take hits the more out-there you become with your Christianity. We suggest you just keep a lid on it. Be who you want to be on weekends and on Sundays when you're not at work, but when you're in front of a camera, don't get into that stuff."

After the meeting, I drove home thinking about the hypocrisy of Hollywood. Later, I wrote my managers this note:

Dear ——

I've done a lot of thinking since our meeting. I thought about everything you said, and here's what I think: In this town you can be a wife-beating, manic-depressive crack-head and everyone opens their arms to you. They say, "Hey, pal, don't worry about it. We'll get you into recovery. It's all part of the journey."

But if you become a born-again Christian and love Jesus Christ and want to share that with other people, they say, "You've committed the

unpardonable sin. You are a bad person. You're intolerant, you're judg-
mental, you're fundamental and that is unacceptable."

I'm sorry, but I am a Christian and I'm not keeping a lid on anything.
I'm not going to go hide in a closet.

—Kirk

It's interesting how Hollywood has taken my decision. I had lunch with a famous scriptwriter and we got into a zesty conversation about how you get to heaven. I told him I was a Christian and he said, "Well, Kirk . . . for an actor in Hollywood, you sure picked the one unacceptable religion, didn't you?"

I turned down the movie *A River Runs Through It* and dozens of other opportunities (much to my manager's disappointment) due to content issues. I remember seeing Leonardo DiCaprio in *Titanic* and thinking, *Little 15-year-old Leonardo is all grown up! What a big hit. What if I had had an opportunity like that? Would I have done this movie?*

Then I thought, *I wouldn't do it. The story is exciting, but it has scenes that I wouldn't touch with a 10-foot pole.*

I turned down one sitcom because I didn't feel right about spending everyday at work, playing husband to another woman and father to other kids. Although that might not seem like a big deal to some, it meant I would live more of life with a make-believe wife and children than with my real family, spending all that time away from Chelsea and the kids. It didn't sit right with me.

Another time, I was offered $100,000 for a quick, easy movie. The story was fun and romantic, but at the end of the movie, my character swept his girlfriend off her feet and plants a big, long, juicy, wet kiss on her. I declined the movie because I had already decided that I would not kiss any woman other than Chelsea. I wasn't trying to make a statement; it was simply my own conviction—one that I'm sure has cost me other opportunities.

Family Audience

One TV historian said, "Some people think Kirk Cameron has hurt his career by being outspoken about his conversion to Christianity. Actually, he's a very smart man. He knows that by playing the Christian hand, he is actually strengthening support from a very large segment of the population. It has helped his career."

What he said about my career still going strong appears to be true. It has changed course, but it's strong. However, being outspoken was not a deliberate choice to help my career; I believed my choice would have the opposite effect, completely tanking my career.

I guess I was wrong. Since then, I've been on VH-1, MTV, Nickelodeon, *ABC Primetime News*, *Larry King* (twice), MSNBC, *Scarborough Country*, *Heartland with John Casik* and the front pages of Yahoo and AOL. I didn't look for these opportunities and no publicity firm could land all these appearances. They've come to me unbidden.

When I was on *The O'Reilly Factor*, Bill asked, "Has your conversion hurt your career in Hollywood?"

I answered, "The truth is, I have a beautiful wife. I've been married 15 years. I've got six kids. I've got an exciting career. I'm passionate about a show I love. And I'm talking to Bill O'Reilly in front of 4 million people, not because I was caught with a gun in my hand but because of my faith. So I think it was a great decision."

For the last 20 years, I've worked hard at developing a trust level with the family audience and it wasn't easy to do. It cost me lots of money and career opportunities. But I feel like the reward is paying off now in other ways and with different opportunities.

Recently I read a script by the people who produced *Facing the Giants*. It was one of the best scripts I've read in a very long time.

I called the producers of the film and told them I was interested in playing the role. They told me that they wanted an actor who could not only play the part, but who was genuinely walking with the Lord. They wanted complete credibility with the Christian world because they wanted pastors to help with the promotion. As they looked for someone to play the role who met their standards, they realized they had very few choices.

They asked me to audition. My manager was shocked. *Didn't they know my work by now? Hadn't they seen me act?*

What we didn't know was that the producers wanted to see me in person, not only to determine if I could handle the emotionally intense role, but to see how I lived out my faith.

These were people who respected my choice to not kiss any woman other than my wife. For one of the final scenes (yes, I got the part), the producers had Chelsea come in, gave her a wig to make her look like the actress who played my wife in the movie, and shot it in silhouette.

The kiss you see is a real kiss with my real bride.

It's funny . . . I've made all the wrong decisions for a lucrative acting career. I've been dropped by UTA, AMG and William Morris agencies. I've made all the wrong decisions, yet 20 years later, I still show up in a positive light on high-profile shows. I'm working on season four of my TV series. And to top it off, my name's written in heaven.

Life is good. The high cost of following Jesus on the narrow road may look totally backward to some, but the infinite value and adventure has been thrilling beyond my wildest dreams.

Chapter 22

From Riches to Rags

I suppose it could be argued that I reached the pinnacle of my success when *Growing Pains* hit its zenith in 1987. But it depends on your definition of success. I am a very wealthy man: I received my riches the day I pulled over to the side of Van Nuys Boulevard and gave my whole self to God—what little I knew of Him at the time.

From the moment I prayed that bumbling prayer, my TV stardom meant nothing. That's not to say, however, that I'm not grateful for the platform. Some say that the only reason we've gotten *The Way of the Master* show on 20 networks is my fame as a teenager. I don't understand why the world listens to me when there are far more articulate teachers and preachers. I guess it's the pull of image and celebrity. Rather than run from it, I've learned to accept it and watch as God uses it for His glory.

I don't mind fans coming to talk to me anymore. I invite it. While I used to walk with my head down, I now walk face-up and look people in the eyes. If they want to stop and chat, great! They push open the door to a conversation and I simply respond with what I'm doing these days.

It took me a while to figure out who I really am. When we were dating, Chelsea occasionally asked, "Who are *you*, Kirk? Because I don't think I'm seeing *you*."

Her question sent me on a discovery mission that has taken years to sort through. And in another 10 years, I might look back at this book and decide I didn't know all that much about myself now. I'm not even 40, for cryin' out loud. But these things I know for sure . . .

- I'm a child of God, a sinner rescued by grace through faith in Jesus Christ. As my pastor once said, "You don't find God—He's not lost. You are, and He finds you."

- I'm Chelsea's husband, protector, partner and friend. After being married for 17 years, I now know she is the most beautiful woman on the planet—inside and out. Chelsea has so many more gifts and talents than I realized when I first met her on the set of *Full House*. She has a deep and beautiful love for God, integrity and character. She is a very inspiring human being. Together, we're learning that love is not a feeling; it's a lifelong commitment. It's a decision to love someone sacrificially, giving yourself for their good.

- I am the father of six spunky children who brighten the world every day they're here. My kids are a never-ending source of joy and challenge. I love spending time with them individually and as a family. It's a privilege to be their father.

- I'm an actor. I love to become part of a story that matters. I love to imagine and play make-believe. Maybe in this, I've never grown up. I may have stumbled into it as a child, but it's a profession I now love. I'm grateful for what I've done so far in show business—and I hope to have the privilege of working as an actor for the rest of my life.

- I'm grateful. I've been blessed with a wonderful mother and father, whose hard work kept our family together during difficult times and who set an example of commitment and forgiveness for us kids. I'm so proud of who my sisters are becoming. Bridgette is a great mom, a committed wife and an absolute hoot to be with. ("You like crystal gel?") Melissa is growing by leaps and bounds in her faith—pressing on to honor Christ—a shining example of a woman who loves her babies and her husband. My little sister, Candace, has her own "full house" with three beautiful bambinos and a great husband—all maturing and growing in their love for family, friends and God.

· I try to be a good friend. I enjoy being a part of others' lives—to be a support when they struggle, to cheer 'em on and share in their joy.

I'm striving to live these roles with excellence. I may not be there yet, but I'm still growing.

If I lost everything tomorrow—and I hope I don't—I pray that my attitude would be the same as Job's. This was a man who went from riches to rags. God allowed everything to be taken away from him as a test of Job's faithfulness. But Job's response tells all:

Though He slay me, yet will I trust in Him (Job 13:15).

As I continue learning, I've realized that everything in this life is temporary. Faith allows me to see Hollywood in its true state, with all its jewels pulled off. Faith shows me better things than the world has to offer and gives me a view of my Savior and His eternal value. Faith lets me climb up above the platform of worldly popularity into heaven to see the priceless treasure of Christ Himself—and now that I've seen Him, I'm uninterested in living for anything less. This is why the Christian says, "I count all things to be loss in view of the surpassing value of knowing Christ Jesus my Lord, for whom I have suffered the loss of all things, and count them but rubbish so that I may gain Christ" (Phil. 3:8). It is my sincere hope that you will know that same joy.[1]

Note

1. Please take the time to read the appendix and recommended reading at the end of this book. I've added them for your benefit because I care about you, your family, and where you'll spend eternity. God bless you.

Perhaps you, like most people, have questions about the existence of God. Maybe you are asking, "Which God is the true God?" and "How do I know Him?"

I've put together a list of resources on my websites (www.Kirk Cameron.com and www.WayOfTheMaster.com) that have been helpful to me in this regard. I encourage you to go and check it out.

Below is a portion of a script Ray Comfort and I wrote for an episode called "Why Christianity?"[1] It addresses how to know the true and living God.

Moral Compass

We know right from wrong because we have a conscience. The conscience is an impartial judge in the courtroom of the mind. It speaks to us irrespective of our will. Its voice can be so powerful that it has driven many men and women to drown themselves in alcohol and some to a faster form of suicide.

Human beings are unique among God's creation in that we are *moral* creatures. That's one of the many things that separate us from the animals. We have a distinctive knowledge of right and wrong, and so we set up court systems with punishment for wrongdoing. Unlike animals, we hold trials in which the evidence for both sides is presented before a jury. We want to ensure that fairness and justice prevail—especially when someone does something wrong against *us*.

Whether we follow it or not, we all have an internal knowledge that it is wrong to lie, steal, murder and commit adultery.

While we don't need to read the Bible to know that it is wrong to murder or that we have a conscience, it is interesting to consider what the all-time bestselling book says regarding this "moral compass." It states that the problem with the human conscience is that it often becomes "seared." That is, it loses its life on the outside and becomes calloused. Like a smoke detector whose batteries are weak, it no longer functions properly. Accordingly, God has designed something to bring the conscience back to life so that it can do its duty. The way to bring life back into the conscience is to look to the moral Law: The Ten Commandments.

The Commandments are like a mirror. When you and I got up this morning, one of the first things we did was look in the mirror. Why did we do that? Because we wanted to see what damage had been done during the night.

The mirror doesn't clean us. All it does is reflect the truth so that we can see ourselves for what we are, and that motivates us to get things fixed up before we go into public.

With that thought in mind, let's look into the mirror of God's moral Law and see what it does to us. It may not be a pretty sight. You may want to look away, but please be patient, because it is a very powerful tool for helping you discover the reality of God's existence.

The Self-Test

The goal in completing this self-examination is to simply stir your conscience so that it will do its God-given duty. If you harden your heart, you will not hear its voice.

First, have you ever told a lie? I'm not talking about using discretion; I'm talking about a bold-faced lie. If you have lied even once, what does that make you? It makes you a liar. The Bible tells us, "Lying lips are an abomination to the LORD" (Prov. 12:22) because He is a God of truth and holiness.

Have you ever stolen anything? The value of the item is irrelevant. If you have, then you are a thief.

Have you ever used God's name in vain? If you have, then you have taken the name of the God who gave you life and used it as a filth word to express disgust. That's called blasphemy, and it's understandably a very serious offense in His sight. (We don't even use the name of Hitler, who killed six million innocent people, as a curse word.) The Bible says that God will not hold him guiltless who takes His name in vain (see Exod. 20:7).

Jesus said, "Everyone who looks at a woman with lust for her has already committed adultery with her in his heart" (Matt. 5:27-28). Have you ever looked with lust at someone other than your spouse? This includes sex outside of marriage.

If you have violated these four Laws, then by your own admission, you are a lying, thieving, blasphemous adulterer at heart, and you have to face God on Judgment Day. And that's only four of the Ten Commandments.

Let's quickly look at the other six.

Is God first in your life, above all else? He should be. He's given you your life and everything that is dear to you. Do you love Him with *all* of your heart, soul, mind and strength? That's the requirement of the First Commandment.

Or have you broken the Second Commandment by making a god in your mind that you're comfortable with—you say, "My god is a loving and merciful god who would never send anyone to hell"? That god doesn't exist; he's a figment of your imagination. To create a god in your mind (your own image of God) is something the Bible calls idolatry. Idolaters will not enter heaven.

Have you always honored your parents absolutely, and kept the Sabbath holy? If not, you have broken the Fourth and Fifth Commandments.

Have you ever hated someone? The Bible says that "everyone who hates his brother is a murderer" (1 John 3:15). Have you coveted (jealously desired) other people's things? This is a violation of the Tenth Commandment.

Here is the crucial question: If God judges you by the moral Law on Judgment Day, will you be found innocent or guilty of breaking this Law? *Think before you answer.* Will you go to heaven or to hell?

Perhaps the thought of going to hell doesn't alarm you, because you don't believe in it. That may be your belief, but if hell exists, your lack of belief won't make it go away. Standing on a freeway and saying, "I don't believe in trucks" won't make the 18-wheeler disappear.

According to recent polls, the majority of Americans *do* believe in a literal place called hell.[2] Most people think that it's a fitting place for Hitler and other mass murderers—and they're right. Because God is good, He will make sure that murderers get what's coming to them. That makes sense.

But God is not only good, He's *perfect*, and His justice is going to be very thorough. God will also punish rapists, adulterers, pedophiles, fornicators, blasphemers, hypocrites, thieves and liars. We are told in the Bible that all liars will have their part in the lake of fire (see Rev. 21:8), and thieves and adulterers will not inherit the kingdom of heaven (see 1 Cor. 6:9). Think about it: If God's standards are that high, that leaves us all in big trouble.

But that's not all. God also sees our *thought-life*, and He will judge us for the hidden sins of the heart: for lust, hatred, rebellion, greed, unclean imaginations, ingratitude, selfishness, jealousy, pride, envy, deceit, and so on. Jesus warned, "But I tell you that *every careless word* that people speak, they shall give an accounting for it in the day of judgment" (Matt. 12:36, emphasis added). The Bible says that God's wrath abides on each of us (see John 3:36) and that every time we sin, we're storing up wrath that will be revealed on Judgment Day (see Rom. 2:5).

Does that concern you? Is your conscience speaking to you? Is it accusing you of being guilty?

Thank you for your patience and honesty with this section—it is a difficult subject to consider. Hopefully your conscience has been awakened. You should now recognize the danger of your predicament. The just penalty of sin—breaking even one Law—is death, and eternity in hell. But you haven't broken just one Law. Like the rest of us, you've no doubt broken all of these laws, countless times each. What kind of anger do you think a judge is justified in having toward a criminal guilty of breaking the Law *thousands of times*?

So what should you do? Turn to religion? But there are so many— which one should you choose? Next we'll look at the answer to this crucial question.

The Four Gifts

Blaise Pascal said, "There are only two kinds of men: the righteous, who believe themselves sinners; the rest, sinners, who believe themselves righteous."

Let's say you are convinced God exists, and you realize you will have to face Him on Judgment Day. But you are not sure which religion to follow to be right with God. Each religion has a different teaching about God, so while they can all be wrong, they can't all be right. Let me show you why Christianity is unique among religions.[3]

Imagine I offered you a choice of four gifts:

1. The original *Mona Lisa*
2. The keys to a brand-new Lamborghini
3. $10 million in cash
4. A parachute

You can pick only one. Which will you choose? Before you decide, here's some information that will help you make the wisest choice: *You have to jump 10,000 feet out of an airplane.*

Does that help you to connect the dots? It should, because you *need* the parachute. It's the only one of the four gifts that will help with your dilemma. The others have some value, but they are useless when it comes to facing the law of gravity and a 10,000-foot fall. The knowledge that you will have to jump should produce a healthy fear in you—and that kind of fear is good, because it can save your life. Remember that.

Now consider four major religions/philosophies:

1. Hinduism
2. Buddhism
3. Islam
4. Christianity

Which one should you choose? Before you decide, here's some information that will help you determine which one is the wisest choice: *All of humanity stands on the edge of eternity.* We are *all* going to die. We will all have to pass through the door of death. It could happen to us in 20 years or in six months . . . or today. For most of humanity, death is a huge and terrifying plummet into the unknown. So what should you do?

Do you remember how it was your knowledge of the law of gravity that produced that healthy fear, and that fear helped you to make the best choice among the four gifts offered above? You know what the law of gravity can do to you from a height of 10,000 feet. In the same way, your knowledge of the moral Law will hopefully help you make the best choice with life's greatest issue: what happens when you die.

The Bible tells us that when we take that "unknown" leap and pass through the door of death, we have to face "the law of sin and death"—the Ten Commandments (see Rom. 8:2; Heb. 9:27). As we have seen, we are without excuse when we stand before God because He gave us our conscience to know right from wrong. Each time we lie, steal, commit adultery, and so on, we know deep inside that what we are doing is wrong.

As we have looked at this subject, you may have developed a sense of fear. Remember to let that fear work for your good. The fear of God is the healthiest fear you can have. The Bible calls it "the beginning of wisdom" (see Ps. 111:10).

Let's look now at those four major religions to see which one, if any, can help you with your predicament.

Hinduism

The religion of Hinduism says that if you've been bad, you may come back as a rat or some other animal.[4] If you've been good, you might come back as a prince. But that's like someone saying, "When you jump out of the plane, you'll get sucked back in as another passenger. If you've been bad, you go down to the Economy Class; if you've been good, you go up to First Class." It's an interesting concept, but it doesn't deal with your real problem of having sinned against God and the reality of hell. And there is no factual evidence for the truthfulness of this belief. (How do you know your great-grandmother came back as a cat?)

Buddhism

Amazingly, some forms of Buddhism deny that God even exists. They declare that life and death are sort of an illusion.[5] That's like standing at the door of the plane and saying, "I'm not really here, and there's no such thing as the law of gravity, and no ground that I'm going to hit."

That may temporarily help you deal with your fears, but it doesn't square with reality. And it doesn't deal with your real problem of having sinned against God and the reality of hell.

Islam

Interestingly, Islam acknowledges the reality of sin and hell, as well as the justice of God, but the hope it offers is that you can escape God's justice if you do religious works. God will see these good works, *and because of them,* hopefully He will show mercy—but you can't know for sure.[6] According to this religion, each person's works will be weighed on the Day of Judgment and it will then be decided who is saved and who is not, based on whether or not they followed Islam, were sincere in repentance and performed enough righteous deeds to outweigh their sins.

Islam believes that you can earn God's mercy by your own efforts. But that's like jumping out of the plane and believing that by flapping your arms, you can overcome the law of gravity and save yourself from a 10,000-foot drop.

And there's something else to consider: The Law of God (the Ten Commandments) shows us that even the best of us is nothing more than a guilty criminal, standing guilty and without excuse before the throne of a perfect and holy Judge. When that is understood, then our "righteous deeds" can actually be seen as an attempt to bribe the Judge of the Universe. The Bible says that because of our guilt, anything we offer God for our justification (to get ourselves off the hook) is an abomination to Him (see Prov. 15:8). Islam, like other works-based religions, cannot save you from the consequences of sinning against God.

Christianity

So why is Christianity different? Aren't all religions the same? Let's see.

In Christianity, God Himself provides a "parachute" for us. The Bible says to "put on the Lord Jesus Christ" (Rom. 13:14). Just as a parachute solved your dilemma with the law of gravity and its consequences, so the Savior perfectly solves your dilemma with the Law of God and its consequences! It is the missing puzzle piece that you need.

How does God solve our dilemma? He satisfied His wrath by becoming a human being and taking our punishment upon Himself. The Scriptures tell us that God was in Christ, reconciling the world to Himself (see 2 Cor. 5:19). Christianity provides the only parachute to save us from the consequences of the Law we have broken.

In looking at the four major religions to see if they can help us in our dilemma, we find that Christianity fits the bill perfectly. To illustrate this more clearly, let's go back to that plane for a moment.

You are standing on the edge of a 10,000-foot drop. You have to jump. Your heart is thumping in your chest. Why? Because you know that the law of gravity will kill you when you jump.

Someone offers you the original Mona Lisa. You push it aside.

Another person passes you the keys to a brand-new Lamborghini. You let them drop to the floor.

Someone else tries to put $10 million into your hands. You push the hand away, and stand there in horror at your impending fate.

Suddenly, you hear a voice say, "Here's a parachute!"

Which one of those four people is going to hold the most credibility in your eyes? It's the one who held up the parachute! Again, it is your knowledge of the law of gravity and your fear of the jump that turns you toward the good news of the parachute.

In the same way, knowledge of what God's moral Law will do to you on the Day of Judgment produces a fear that makes the gospel unspeakably good news! It solves your predicament of God's wrath. God became a sinless human being in the person of Jesus of Nazareth. The Savior died an excruciating death on the cross, taking your punishment (the death penalty) upon Himself, and the demands of eternal justice were satisfied the moment He cried, "It is finished!" The Bible tells us, "Christ redeemed us from the curse of the Law, having become a curse for us" (Gal. 3:13). We broke the Law, but God became a man to pay our penalty with His own life's blood.

Then He rose from the dead, defeating death. This means that God can forgive every sin you have ever committed and cancel your death sentence. When you repent (turn from your sins) and place your faith in Jesus Christ, you can say with the apostle Paul: "For the law of the

Spirit of life in Christ Jesus has set you free from the law of sin and of death" (Rom. 8:2).

You no longer need to be afraid of death, and you don't need to look any further for ways to make peace between you and God. The Savior is God's gift to you. He is truly good news! Now God Himself can "justify" you. He can wash you clean and give you the "righteousness" of Christ. He can save you from death and hell, and grant you everlasting life—something that you could never earn or deserve.

So if you haven't yet repented and trusted the Savior, please do it now. Simply tell God you are sorry for your sins, then *turn* from them and place your trust in Jesus Christ alone to save you. Don't wait until tomorrow. It may never come.

He Made a Way

The Bible tells us that this same Judge who will find you guilty of breaking His Law is also rich in mercy. He has made a way for you to be forgiven. "For God so loved the world, that He gave His only begotten Son, that whoever believes in Him shall not perish, but have eternal life" (John 3:16).

If there is one chance in a million that this is true, then you owe it to your good sense to consider it with an open heart. God offers everlasting life to all humanity and promises, "Their sins and their lawless deeds I will remember no more" (Heb. 10:17). What you must do in response is to "repent" (not simply confess your sins, but *turn* from them) and trust the Savior (not just a belief, but a "trust"—as you would trust a parachute to save you). The moment you do that, God reveals Himself to you—not necessarily in a vision or in a voice, but by giving you His Holy Spirit to live inside of you. He makes you brand new on the inside, so that you want to do what is pleasing to Him.

That's a miracle for a sin-loving sinner. It's so radical that the Bible calls it being "born again."

It's like this: If I look at a heater and *believe* the heater is hot, I have an intellectual belief. But if I say to myself, "I wonder if it really *is* hot" and reach out and grip the bar, the second my flesh burns, I stop *believing* it's hot—I now *know* it's hot. I have moved out of the realm of *belief* into the realm of *experience*.

That's what will happen to you the moment you are born again (when you become a Christian). You will move out of the realm of "belief" into the realm of "personal experience." A Christian is not someone who has a belief, but someone who has a relationship with the living God. You come to *know* Him. You will say with the writer of "Amazing Grace," "I once was blind, but now I see."

Notes

1. From Ray Comfort, *How to Know God Exists* (Alachua, FL: Bridge Logos Publishers, 2008). Used by permission of Bridge Logos Publishers.
2. Frank Newport, "Americans More Likely to Believe in God than the Devil, Heaven More than Hell," Gallup News Service, June 13, 2007. http://www.gallup.com/poll/27877/Americans-More-Likely-Believe-God-Than-Devil-Heaven-More-Than-Hell.aspx (accessed January 2008).
3. A condensed version of this chapter, called *Why Christianity?*, is available in booklet form. See www.livingwaters.com.
4. "Is it possible for a man to be reborn as a lower animal?" Maharshi: "Yes. It is possible, as illustrated by Jada Bharata—the scriptural anecdote of a royal sage having been reborn as a deer." From *The Teaching of Sri Ramana Maharishi*, edited by David Godman. www.hinduism.co.za/reincarn.htm (accessed January 2008).
5. "When you transcend your thinking mind in the realization of your own pure, timeless, ever-present awareness, then the illusion of time completely collapses, and you become utterly free of the samsaric cycle of time, change, impermanence, and suffering." Tom Huston, "Buddhism and the Illusion of Time." http://www.buddhistinformation.com/buddhism_and_the_illusion_of_time.htm (accessed January 2008).
6. "Then those whose balance (of good deeds) is heavy, they will be successful. But those whose balance is light, will be those who have lost their souls; in hell will they abide" (Sura 23:102-103).

Recommended Reading

This is a short list of books that I highly recommend.

On the Existence of God

Comfort, Ray. *God Doesn't Believe in Atheists: Proof that the Atheist Does Not Exist.* Alachua, FL: Bridge Logos Publishers, revised edition, 1993.

D'Souza, Dinesh. *What's So Great About Christianity.* Washington, DC: Regnery Publishing, Inc., 2007.

Geisler, Norman L., and Frank Turek. *I Don't Have Enough Faith to Be an Atheist.* Wheaton, IL: Crossway Books, 2004.

Strobel, Lee. *The Case for a Creator: A Journalist Investigates Scientific Evidence that Points Toward God.* Grand Rapids, MI: Zondervan, new edition, 2005.

On True Christianity

Alcorn, Randy. *Heaven.* Carol Stream, IL: Tyndale House Publishers, 2004.

——. *Money, Possessions and Eternity.* Carol Stream, IL: Tyndale House Publishers, rev. ed. 2003.

——. *Safely Home.* Carol Stream, IL: Tyndale House Publishers, 2003.

Comfort, Ray. *The Way of the Master.* Alachua, FL: Bridge Logos Publishers, 2006.

MacArthur, John. *The MacArthur Study Bible (NASB).* Nashville, TN: Nelson Bibles, 2006. Read every verse and every footnote in the New Testament (at your own pace) and you will have a firm foundation.

——. *Hard to Believe: The High Cost and Infinite Value of Following Jesus.* Nashville, TN: Thomas Nelson Publishers, 2003.

Mahaney, C. J. *The Cross Centered Life: Keeping the Gospel the Main Thing.* Colorado Springs, CO: Multnomah, 2002.

Meade, Matthew. *The Almost Christian Discovered.* Lake Mary, FL: Soli Deo Gloria Ministries, 1997.

Classics Every Christian Should Read

Bunyan, John. *The Pilgrim's Progress.* New York: Oxford University Press, new ed., 2003.

Foxe, John. *Foxe's Book of Martyrs.* Gainesville, FL: Bridge-Logos, 2001.

Spurgeon, Charles. *Lectures to My Students.* Grand Rapids, MI: Zondervan, new ed., 1979.

——. *Morning and Evening.* Crossway Books, rev. ed., 2003.

——. *The Soul Winner.* Grand Rapids, MI: Wm. B. Eerdmans Publishing Co., rev. ed., 1995.

Tozer, A. W. *The Pursuit of God.* Camp Hill, PA: Christian Publications, Inc., 1993.

Camp Firefly, like any other grass-roots effort, relies on generous people to continue. We do not take any pay for what we do, but the camp itself needs funding. If you would like to help these families by donating in-kind gifts or financially sponsoring a portion of Camp Firefly, write to:

The Firefly Foundation
5737 Kanan Road #180
Agoura, CA 91301

A DVD with more information about Camp Firefly is available from the same address. Please also visit our website at www.CampFirefly.com.

More Great Resources
from Regal

The Truth Comes Out
When Someone You Love
Is in a Same-Sex Relationship
Nancy Heche
ISBN 978.08307.39122

**Through a
Screen Darkly**
Looking Closer at Beauty,
Truth and Evil in the Movies
Jeffrey Overstreet
ISBN 978.08307.43154

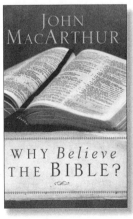

Why Believe the Bible?
John MacArthur
ISBN 978.08307.45647

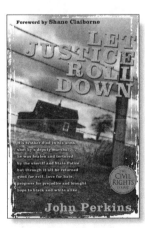

Let Justice Roll Down
The Civil Rights Classic
John Perkins
ISBN 978.08307.43073

Available at Bookstores Everywhere!

From Lost Boy to World-Renowned Evangelist and Pastor

Growning up in a dysfunctional family, Greg Laurie knew what it was to be lost. But when he discovered a passion for seeing people rescued from hopelessness and transformed into renewed beings in Christ, he quickly became a wonder and an example as to how God could use someone with a sordid past to impact the world with the gospel. The Lord's influence in Greg's life has been thoroughly evidenced by the fruit seen from the ministries he has planted, including Harvest Christian Fellowship and the Harvest Crusades. If God can take a hippie and raise him to be one of the nation's leading evangelists, what can He do with you?

Lost Boy:
My Story
Greg Laurie with
Ellen Vaughn
ISBN 978.08307.45784

Available at Bookstores Everywhere!